Public Libraries and Marxism

Public Libraries and Marxism provides a Marxist analytical framework for understanding public libraries and presents a set of proposals for transforming the capitalist libraries of today.

Evaluating the strengths and weaknesses of this Marxist framework, the authors also provide a critical examination of the history, theory and practice of libraries in the Soviet Union and North Korea. Considering what a Marxist library service would look like in the Western capitalist countries of today, Pateman and Pateman synthesise the insights provided throughout the book into a set of Marxist proposals designed to promote the transformation of contemporary Western public librarianship. These proposals suggest how Western public libraries can change their organisation and practices – their strategies, structures, systems and culture – in order to best serve those with the most needs, particularly as society evolves in response to new challenges.

Public Libraries and Marxism will be relevant for scholars and students of library and information science, history, politics and sociology. Outlining the rudiments of a Marxist library service that should be applicable around the world, the book will also appeal to library practitioners who want to develop libraries in a community-led and needs-based direction.

Joe Pateman is a doctoral candidate in politics at the University of Nottingham, UK. Joe's research interests include Marxism-Leninism, democratic theory and the political economy of race. Joe is the co-author of *Managing Cultural Change in Public Libraries: Marx, Maslow, and Management* (2019, Routledge).

John Pateman is Chief Executive Officer and Chief Librarian of Thunder Bay Public Library in Thunder Bay, Ontario, Canada. He was previously Head of Libraries in Hackney, Merton and Lincolnshire in the UK. He is the joint author of *Public Libraries and Social Justice* (2010, Routledge), *Developing Community Led Public Libraries* (2013, Routledge) and *Managing Cultural Change in Public Libraries: Marx, Maslow, and Management* (2019, Routledge).

Public Libraries and Marxism

Joe Pateman and John Pateman

LONDON AND NEW YORK

First published 2021
by Routledge
2 Park Square, Milton Park, Abingdon, Oxon OX14 4RN

and by Routledge
605 Third Avenue, New York, NY 10158

Routledge is an imprint of the Taylor & Francis Group, an informa business

© 2021 Joe Pateman and John Pateman

The right of Joe Pateman and John Pateman to be identified as authors of this work has been asserted by them in accordance with sections 77 and 78 of the Copyright, Designs and Patents Act 1988.

All rights reserved. No part of this book may be reprinted or reproduced or utilised in any form or by any electronic, mechanical, or other means, now known or hereafter invented, including photocopying and recording, or in any information storage or retrieval system, without permission in writing from the publishers.

Trademark notice: Product or corporate names may be trademarks or registered trademarks, and are used only for identification and explanation without intent to infringe.

British Library Cataloguing-in-Publication Data
A catalogue record for this book is available from the British Library

Library of Congress Cataloging-in-Publication Data
Names: Pateman, Joe, author. | Pateman, John, 1956– author.
Title: Public libraries and Marxism / Joe Pateman and John Pateman.
Description: Milton Park, Abingdon, Oxon ; New York, NY : Routledge, 2022. | Includes bibliographical references and index.
Identifiers: LCCN 2021008390 (print) | LCCN 2021008391 (ebook) | ISBN 9780367761073 (hardback) | ISBN 9780367761196 (paperback) | ISBN 9781003165545 (ebook)
Subjects: LCSH: Public libraries—Administration. | Libraries and communism. | Libraries—Soviet Union—History—20th century. | Libraries—Korea (North)—History—20th century. | Libraries and society. | Critical theory.
Classification: LCC Z678 .P295 2022 (print) | LCC Z678 (ebook) | DDC 025.1/974—dc23
LC record available at https://lccn.loc.gov/2021008390
LC ebook record available at https://lccn.loc.gov/2021008391

ISBN: 978-0-367-76107-3 (hbk)
ISBN: 978-0-367-76119-6 (pbk)
ISBN: 978-1-003-16554-5 (ebk)

Typeset in Times New Roman
by Apex CoVantage, LLC

This book is dedicated to the memory of Vladimir Lenin (1870–1924). His ideas inspired and motivated us to write this book.

As soon as the proletariat began to think practically, the first thing they did was start reading and organizing libraries. This fact is highly distinctive and characteristic of our revolution, and not only of the October Revolution but of the entire working-class movement.

– M. N. Pokrovsky

Contents

	Acknowledgements	viii
1	Introduction	1
2	The Marxist interpretation of the public library	20
3	V. I. Lenin and the Soviet socialist public library system	44
4	Kim Il-Sung and socialist public libraries in North Korea	71
5	The Vanguard library	92
6	Conclusion	117
	Index	120

Acknowledgements

We would like to acknowledge the valuable support, advice and guidance that we received from Heidi Lowther, our editor at Routledge, who helped us strengthen and focus the analysis in this book.

1 Introduction

A book called *Public Libraries and Marxism* may elicit surprise or even derision in some quarters. Aren't the two traditions hostile to one another? Is a 'Marxist public library' not an oxymoron? Yet one more bizarre product of Marxism's search for a dialectical 'unity of opposites'? For many public librarians today, Marxism could not be more irrelevant to their discipline. In mainstream discourse, it is portrayed as an authoritarian creed of a bygone era, a quasi-religion responsible for creating a totalitarian system of mass murder and tyranny. Marxism is routinely blamed for the alleged repressions and crimes committed by power-hungry communists under the rule of alleged 'despots' like Stalin, Mao and their followers in the other one-party socialist regimes. Under the guidance of Marxism, the public libraries in the socialist countries supposedly functioned as crude propaganda organs. They violated the principles of free expression, non-partisanship and uncensored knowledge, principles that Western librarians supposedly hold dear to their hearts (Sroka 2013; Anghelescu 2001; Șerbănuță 2017; Mostecky 1956; Kase 1961; Kosciejew 2009a, 2009b). After the collapse of Soviet communism in 1990, many concluded that Marxism lost any remaining significance for public librarianship. The once-popular ideology is supposedly dead and beyond resurrection. It consists of a set of dogmatic, non-challengeable postulates, which have been discredited by history and which have no useful application for public libraries today. The few devotees who continue to promote Marxism are derided as relics from a prehistoric era: living dinosaurs whose rigid, formulaic, outdated dogmas have little value for contemporary public librarianship. So the common story goes.

Why, then, study the Marxist theory and practice of public librarianship today? There are obvious historical reasons. Whatever one thinks of Marxism, it is *undeniable* that it has been hugely influential upon the modern history of public libraries. At the height of its influence, Marxist public libraries served nearly half the world's population in socialist countries. These once included the Soviet Union, Bulgaria, Yugoslavia,

2 Introduction

Czechoslovakia, Hungary, Albania, East Germany, Poland and Romania. Today, socialist public libraries continue to grow and develop in the worlds remaining socialist countries: China, Cuba, Vietnam, Laos and North Korea (Harris and Creamer 1996). Among these, China is set to supplant the US as the world's leading geopolitical and economic superpower. The common claim that these socialist states have 'abandoned' Marxism for capitalism is a bourgeois myth, designed to discredit their achievements. It is based on the erroneous notion that Marxism is incapable of evolving over time. In fact, Marxism is the enemy of all dogmatism, and the remaining socialist states have survived precisely because they have grasped this fact (Pateman 2019). China, Cuba, Vietnam, Laos and North Korea are Marxist states. Their public libraries are based wholly on Marxism. It is therefore impossible to understand the world of public librarianship without understanding the world of Marxist public librarianship. To ignore Marxism is to remain with a limited, narrow, Western-centric view of public libraries, one that cannot claim to be authoritative. One of the aims of this book is to illuminate the rich and detailed history of Marxist public librarianship in socialist countries. This history has been neglected and caricatured by prejudiced Western scholars for too long. The hostile 'cold war' attitude to the socialist states must be overcome.

But what about the relevance of Marxism for public libraries in Western capitalist countries, the nations governed by liberalism rather than Marxism? Another aim of this book is to challenge the notion that Marxism is irrelevant in the West. By developing a Marxist framework for understanding public libraries, one that is based on the experience of the socialist countries, it argues that Marxism is not only relevant for understanding public libraries in the West today but also *essential* for doing so. Marxism provides a unique insight into the history, theory and practice of Western public librarianship. It provides a powerful critique and exposé of liberalism, the dominant bourgeois ideology of Western public libraries today. Moreover, this book argues that Marxism can also help create a Western public library service that truly serves the public in all its diversity. Marxism shows that the public library ought to serve the needs of the working class, the majority. It shows, moreover, that the public library can achieve this purpose only in a society in which the workers reign supreme. The public library systems in socialist states provide a great deal of experience in this regard. By abolishing capitalism and beginning the construction of socialism, they made substantial progress in developing a public library service for the people. These systems have not provided perfect services for the workers. On the contrary, they have faced, and continue to face, several shortcomings. Nevertheless, this book argues that they offer valuable lessons on how to create workers' libraries. By drawing on their experiences, it develops a guide for creating a genuine working-class library today. That is why this book is relevant for all those public librarians seeking to truly serve the working class, the public.

Some may choose to see this argument as an endorsement of the one-party socialist state, along with all the 'evils' they have supposedly brought: tyranny, murder, oppression, pervasive censorship. This would be a mistaken interpretation. The purpose of this book is simply to demonstrate the link between the public library and working-class liberation, on one hand, and the necessity of using Marxism to highlight this link, on the other. This book does not claim that the one-party state is the only political framework for developing a workers' public library. It simply recognises the plain fact that they have come the closest to developing such a library. In the future, different socialist systems may well develop workers' public libraries in areas where one-party regimes have failed.

This argument is bound to upset those cold-war liberals who view the socialist countries as bastions of totalitarianism and who insist that the public libraries there violated everything that the service should stand for. They will shout in unison that libraries should be non-partisan and that Marxism is incompatible with the values of public librarianship. Others – claiming to be Marxists – will argue that the socialist countries have nothing in common with Marxism and that libraries there are governed not by Marxism but by totalitarianism. Both views reduce complex issues to crude dichotomies: Marxism is either responsible for creating a repressive library system, which has no redeeming features, or it has no relation whatsoever with this system. Both views fail to appreciate how the objective conditions affect the practical application of theories. On one hand, it is absurd to blame Marxism for every 'negative' feature of the socialist library system, and there are many. But it is equally absurd to delink Marxism from the socialist library system entirely. This system is founded on Marxism.

Having established the basic argument of this book, it is now time to deal with a preliminary question: How does this book define the key terms, *Marxism* and *public library*?

Marxism

Marxism is a communist ideology created by Karl Marx and Frederick Engels, who are known, within the tradition, as the 'founders', or 'classics'. Marx and Engels outlined the essential principles of Marxism in several writings, most notably *The Communist Manifesto*, *Capital* and *Socialism: Utopian and Scientific*.

Despite its global influence, the meaning of Marxism is fiercely contested (Claeys 2018). Although the classical works are well known, there is little agreement over what ideas they express and endorse. The writings of Marx and Engels have been interpreted, applied and developed in a variety of ways. As such, when people speak of 'Marxism', they really mean a specific interpretation of it, one derived either wholly or partially from the classical texts. There are numerous variants and sub-variants of Marxism, all of which claim to be the genuine article. Since there are so many, its adherents have tended to dispute amongst themselves as much as disputing other doctrines. It is therefore necessary to be wary when someone or something is described as 'Marxist'. It could mean a whole variety of things, some of which may not be accepted as 'Marxist' by others (see Kolakowski 2005).

It is frequently the case that writers do not bother defining and distinguishing their interpretation of Marxism. This has become a convenient method of stealthily inserting non-Marxist ideas into the doctrine. This book is more transparent and honest. It unapologetically endorses the interpretation of Marxism called *Marxism-Leninism*, which has guided the theory and practice of the socialist regimes identified earlier (Kuusinen 1961). The fundamentals of Marxism-Leninism were clarified by V. I. Lenin, the founder of the Russian Communist Party and the leader of the 1917 October Socialist Revolution. Marxism-Leninism has been applied differently in the socialist states in accordance with their specific conditions. Nevertheless, it does contain essential features, which are explored more thoroughly in the following chapters:

1 *Dialectical Materialism:* an ontology that explains the composition and development of the world. It is composed of 'materialism' and 'dialectics'. Materialism maintains that matter determines consciousness; that the environmental conditions shape people's ideas. Materialism is the opposite of 'idealism', which maintains that consciousness determines matter and that people's ideas shape their environments. Dialectics views the world as being interconnected and in a constant state of motion. It is the opposite of metaphysics, which identifies unchangeable, unconnected, immutable objects in the world. Dialectics maintains that natural and social phenomena develop in accordance with three universal laws of motion: (1) the law of the unity and conflict of opposites, (2) the law of the passage of quantitative changes into qualitative changes and (3) the law of the negation of the negation. The first law expresses the idea that phenomena contain internal contradictions that drive their development. To take a basic example, in biological evolution, the formation of new forms of life occurs through the unity and struggle of opposites in heredity and variability. The second law describes how incremental changes lead to wholesale transformations. The phase transition of water into ice through cooling is an example

of this. Finally, the third law describes how new phenomena inherit the useful aspects of the old whilst also taking on new characteristics. In evolution, for instance, new species retain some biological aspects from their ancestors whilst also having new features. As an epistemology, dialectical materialism emphasises that the truth is 'concrete'. Propositions can be valid only in relation to a specific environment and time. Dialectical materialism therefore rejects the existence of absolute truths and universal dogmas.

2 *Historical Materialism:* a methodology for understanding society, derived from dialectical materialism. It divides society into its 'base' and 'superstructure'. The economic base comprises (a) the 'productive forces', which include the raw materials used in production and the facilities and instruments used to process these materials (called the 'means of production'), as well as the labourers themselves, and (b) the 'relations of production', the social relations between those in involved in the production process. The superstructure contains everything else, most notably the dominant political, ideological and cultural features of the mode of production. The economic base has causal primacy. It shapes and determines the superstructure. Historical materialism views the historical development of society as a teleological process, one possessing a beginning, middle and end. This development is dictated by the objective laws of dialectical materialism, which manifest themselves in an economic form.

3 *Class Analysis:* the view of society as a structure of hierarchically arranged, inherently antagonistic classes, differentiated on the basis of their position and function in the organisation of production.

4 *Scientific Communism:* the theory that the working class will abolish capitalism and establish the 'dictatorship of the proletariat', a socialist society in which the workers reign supreme. After doing that, the workers will build communism, a classless, stateless society of material abundance. This theory is 'scientific' because it views communism as the inevitable product of structural economic development. It results not from the right ideas or utopian blueprints but from the inexorable logic of objective dialectical laws.

5 *Vanguardism:* the doctrine that the working class can emancipate itself only under the leadership of a revolutionary organisation armed with Marxist theory. This organisation is known as the 'vanguard'.

(Kuusinen 1961)

There are several reasons why this book endorses Marxism-Leninism, a variant of Marxism that has been demonised in the West. The first is that Marxism-Leninism provides the truest, most faithful interpretation of

Marxism. It adheres more consistently to the teachings of Marx and Engels whilst updating and enriching them for modern times (Kuusinen 1961).

The second reason is that Marxism-Leninism has had the most practical success in the field of public librarianship. No other 'Marxism' has established itself as the guiding ideology of a national public library service. Since this book examines the interrelation of Marxist public library theory *and* practice, Marxism-Leninism provides the richest insights in that regard.

Third, and this will be made clearer later on, Marxism-Leninism provides the deepest, most illuminating analysis of public libraries. Besides highlighting the essence of the phenomenon, it provides the key to creating a truly revolutionary working-class public library service. No other 'Marxism' has achieved these objectives. No other 'Marxism' can achieve these objectives. These are the reasons why Marxism-Leninism was chosen.

The public library

At a first glance, the essence and purpose of the public library appear to be obvious and in no need of elaboration. It is one of the most widespread public services in the twenty-first century. There is hardly anyone who has no knowledge of it, who would not have an idea about what it should be like or how its services should be delivered and developed. As such, even many library academics do not even bother defining it. They simply take for granted that its meaning is widely recognised and uncontested. Indeed, the term suggests one, seemingly simple thing – that the library is 'public'. The purpose of putting the word *public* before *library* is to signal that not only is the service *for* the public, the people, but that it is also in some sense controlled *by* the public, the people.

But what is the public? Who does it consist of? How does it use the library? What is a library? What are the criteria of a public library? Whose interests does it serve? The leaders of the various classes in different ages have given opposed answers to these questions. The socialist countries also describe some of their libraries as 'public', and it is not difficult to see that they imbue the term with a meaning quite different from that held in the Western world. Does this mean that the public library is a relativistic term that has a different meaning for everyone? No, it does not mean this. The three main interpretations of the public library can be typified.

The first and original interpretation was formulated in ancient times. It defines the public library as a cultural expression of class power. Whilst analysing the rise of the Greek, Egyptian and Roman empires, observers recognised that public libraries were not simply repositories of information but also manifestations of class domination. This interpretation carried on through feudal times and into the capitalist era. In the mid-nineteenth century, bourgeois reformers promoted public libraries in order to exclude and pacify the working class, on one hand, and to cater to the middle classes, on the other. Then, with the rise of twentieth-century socialism, the ruling communist parties promoted public libraries in order to empower and emancipate the working class, the majority. This original interpretation of the public library as a form of class power, specifically the cultural power of the working masses, constitutes the basis of the Marxist approach to public libraries.

A second interpretation of the public library was shaped by bourgeois reformists in the mid-nineteenth century, during the rise of industrial capitalism. The essence of this interpretation is that the public library is merely an *information provider*. It deliberately disregards the question of *whose* rule is embodied in the institution, and it concentrates primarily on *the way the service is delivered*. It presents the library as an apolitical, neutral, classless institution, one that provides its services to everyone equally, without discrimination (Edwards 1859, 1864; Murison 1988). This interpretation has become so widespread that today it has the dominant influence among the bourgeois interpretations of the public library. Its adherents typically highlight five features shared by public libraries, which basically characterise the ones in the Western capitalist democracies: (1) they are generally supported by taxes; (2) they are governed by a board to serve the public interest; (3) they are open to all; (4) they are voluntary, meaning that no one is forced to use them; and (5) they provide basic services gratis (Rubin 2010).

A third interpretation of the public library broadens the concept into a category that surpasses the cultural sphere and which is completely general, comprehensive and positive. It figured primarily as the propaganda slogan of the mid-nineteenth-century bourgeois reformers who, 'in defence of public libraries', attacked the anti-democratic, exclusive character of the capitalist state and its institutions. It was during this period that the public libraries became associated with noble ideals like 'democracy', 'freedom', 'diversity' and 'inclusion'. This interpretation has since become widespread amongst librarians in capitalist countries (Kranich 2001). Take, for example, the following statement from the Canadian Urban Libraries Council, which represents the large public library systems in Canada:

> Twenty-first century libraries are pillars of safety, inclusion, diversity and democracy for the communities we serve. Libraries provide equitable access to information and digital resources for all people, regardless of race. They provide safe, respectful and welcoming spaces for civic discourse and the expression of diverse voices. Through carefully curated collections, community partnerships and targeted outreach, libraries intentionally engage and serve the needs of all populations.

And, increasingly, libraries are taking bold stands and speaking up to call out and combat social injustice.

(Benton 2020)

The UK government promoted similar ideals in its corporate report, *Libraries Deliver: Ambition for Public Libraries in England 2016 to 2021* (GOV n.d.). Amongst other things, the report associates public libraries with the promotion of 'cultural and creative enrichment', 'helping everyone achieve their full potential', 'healthier and happier lives', 'greater prosperity' and 'stronger, more resilient communities'. These ideals are being promoted by a Tory government that has systematically cut public library funding over the past decade. Hiding behind the neo-liberal mask of 'austerity politics' the Conservatives, and their Liberal Democrat partners, closed hundreds of public libraries and laid off thousands of library workers in the wake of the 2008 financial crisis.

This third interpretation of the public library has not become as general as the second one, which considers it to be a neutral information provider. This is due partly to the traditions of library science and partly to the fact that the adherents of this third conception are greatly divided.

As can be seen from this examination of the three interpretations of the public library, instead of giving a definition of this cultural category, the historical representatives of librarianship often describe only certain aspects of it (e.g. type two, forms of information provision) or only some of its consequences (that is the situation in the case of the third interpretation). Instead of the question, 'What is the public library?' they answer the question, 'What characterises the public library?' Naturally, the characteristics of the public library cannot be separated from the object of which they are manifestations. However, in spite of this, there are two different levels in question. 'What is the public library?' is a question about the essence, and the answer given to it separates differing political and class standpoints. 'What characterises the public library?' is a question the answer to which is given by referring to phenomena determined by these standpoints. These two levels, namely that of the essence and that of the phenomena, must not be confused.

Over the course of history, the concept of the public library has gradually become empty. This has come about in two main ways: on one hand, the public library has been restricted to forms of information provision only, while, on the other hand, its consequences have been extended and exaggerated so much that it has become difficult to interpret the term. The result, however, has been the same in both cases. The word *public library* has lost its original class connotation, and it is not consistent with its etymology. Namely it does not serve the public, the working masses, but instead, it has become a means of pacifying and excluding the masses.

Nevertheless, this typology has several uses. First, it convincingly proves that *there is no public library in general*; *every public library is concrete* and is a cultural practice – and theoretical category – related to a definite age and a definite class.

Second, a typology of the various interpretations of the public library also proves that they derive not from individual differences but from class differences. Consequently, the typical interpretations represent definite social standpoints. That is, they always reflect – more or less accurately – real class relations. That is why these interpretations are not subjective and inconceivable abstractions. They are based on the reflection of reality.

Finally, in the course of making this typology, *the various actual (or supposed) aspects of the public library become clear*. This makes it possible to get a more precise picture of the public library reflected differently in the consciousness of the various classes, to discover the proper place of this phenomenon in social life and, by this, to acquire a more adequate knowledge of it. That is one of the aims of this book.

The critical scholarship on public libraries

Having established the meaning of 'Marxism' and the 'public library', it is now useful, before outlining the book's structure, to show its relation to the recent scholarship on public libraries. Doing so can help clarify the main argument and its contribution to the literature.

Marxism, in capitalist countries, is categorised as a *critical* perspective. It critically examines the prevailing order and its dominant discourse; it exposes how these maintain oppression, and it identifies alternatives. Marxism is not alone in this regard. Several other theories do the same thing. Critical perspectives have a relatively small presence in library science, however. This should be unsurprising, considering the age-old association of librarianship with liberalism and conservatism, the preservation of the status quo. Nevertheless, a small scholarship has brought (1) intersectionality, (2) critical theory and (3) Western Marxism to bear on the dominant theories and practices of libraries. The following sections examine these three approaches in turn.

Intersectionality

Intersectionality is a popular concept that emerged in academic discourse relatively recently (Eisenstein 2018). It highlights the fact that some people experience multiple, overlapping forms of oppression. Black women, for instance, are oppressed not only as blacks but as women too. Intersectionality has been successful in raising the consciousness of marginalised groups and drawing them into social and political action for the first time in their lives. As such, it forms a potential bridge into the class struggle. This makes intersectionality an insightful concept, one that Marxists should not ignore. It can help remind them that the working class is a *diverse* class. It faces not only economic exploitation but racial, gender and other forms of oppression too.

That said, intersectionality does not help the emancipatory struggle. This is so because it gives the various forms of oppression equal weight. Intersectionality gives no particular source more power than others. As such, class oppression is simply represented as another form of oppression, alongside others like race and gender. By doing this, intersectionality fails to recognise that the class system is an objective structure conditioning and maintaining the other forms of oppression. The class system did not create racism and sexism, but it is a structural barrier to overcoming them. By denying the primacy of class, intersectionality fails to rally the masses against capitalism. It turns the workers' attention away from the class structure and towards the other forms of oppression. This has resulted – perhaps against the wishes of some intersectionality theorists – in dividing the working class into separate *identity politics* movements, some of which are hostile to one another. Male workers have been set against women workers, black workers have been set against white workers and so on and so forth. This fragmentation and infighting have, of course, weakened, rather than strengthened, the working class as a whole. Instead of uniting the working class, intersectionality has divided it into competing tribal factions (Eisenstein 2018; McGarvey 2017). That is why intersectionality cannot be an effective theory of emancipation. As the following review shows, the studies that apply intersectionality to libraries suffer from this drawback.

The edited collection *Feminists Among Us* considers resistance and advocacy in library leadership. All the contributors are feminists, 'bringing to their accounts varied experiences of gender discrimination intersected with race, class, sexuality, and other social categories that are oppressed in patriarchal systems of power and organization' (Lew and Yousefi 2017: 2). While class is recognised as one of the key intersectional 'identities', it is regarded as equivalent to them, rather than as a causal factor shaping them. Also, class and the other identities are not viewed through a Marxist lens but via 'critical theory frameworks' and 'feminist critical theories'.

Race as an identity is examined in a similar way in *Topographies of Whiteness: Mapping Whiteness in Library and Information Science*. In doing so, the authors of this collected edition 'speak to the relationship between whiteness and gender, neoliberalism, and . . . diversity and social justice' (Schlesselman-Tarango 2017: 2). Once again, the focus is on how identities intersect. But in place of Marxism, 'the structures of "imperialism, capitalism and white supremacy" are explored through the prism of "critical whiteness studies"'. Whiteness as a social construction is elevated above class, which is economically determined, although it is conceded that

> [w]hile it would be difficult to argue against the value of intersectional analysis . . . some warn against lingering in specificity and instead point to the need to explore the ways in which whiteness is produced and operates across age, gender, sex, class and the like
> (Schlesselman-Tarango 2017: 12–13)

The dangers of 'specificity' and of taking a too narrowly focused identity-based approach are also recognised in *Pushing the Margins: Women of Color and Intersectionality in LIS*:

> There are many valid critiques of intersectionality and its limits. . . . Some of these critiques include the risk of essentialism – by studying identities as categories, we can end up reproducing and re-emphasizing them. . . . Rather than focusing on individual social categories, we need to seek and challenge the power structures that enable interlocking systems of oppression.
> (Chou and Pho 2018: 4)

Class, however, is not identified within this context, and the authors of this collected edition eschew Marxism in favour of 'critical, feminist, and queer theory' and 'critical librarianship' (Chou and Pho 2018: 6). At the same time, the inadequacy of critical librarianship is also recognised. As Brown et al. succinctly point out,

> [e]ven more troubling is that the movement does not seem to want to turn a critical eye upon itself or the profession, focusing mostly on critically engaging with the work librarians do, such as instruction, reference, or cataloguing. It does not, for example, question the fact that the profession is replicating structures of white supremacy in LIS [library and information science] curriculum, programs, recruitment, and the culture of the profession.
> (Brown et al. 2018: 173)

By utilising intersectionality, the contributors to these volumes succeed in highlighting the various overlapping forms of racial and gender oppression in the public library. They fail, however, in recognising the primacy of class oppression, and this failure derives from their dependence on intersectionality. Despite their wishes, they cater to state monopoly capitalism by promoting identity politics as the way forward for public libraries, rather than the class struggle. Marxism-Leninism does not make that mistake. It correctly identifies the class system as the primary barrier to emancipation. Whilst acknowledging the significance of racial, gender and other forms of oppression, it recognises that these can only be overcome through a united class struggle against capitalism. That is what makes Marxism-Leninism an effective theory of emancipation. By utilising Marxism-Leninism, this book maintains that the public library needs to focus its efforts on tackling class oppression. The public library must serve the working class in all its diversity.

Critical theory

Critical theory highlights the role of ideology and culture in maintaining oppressive power structures in society (Guess 1991). It views ideas and beliefs as the main barriers to emancipation. Critical theorists reject what they call the 'scientific method' in favour of a range of other methodologies, such as psychoanalysis. As a result, the tradition is a mixed bag of perspectives rather than a single, coherent standpoint. Some critical theorists denounce particular Marxist concepts or combine Marxism with other sociological and philosophical traditions. Others associated with critical theory reject Marxism entirely (Held 2004).

The main strength of critical theory is its recognition that *ideas* play an important part in sustaining oppression. Some Marxists have rightly been criticised for neglecting the significance of ideas whilst focusing on economic factors. Critical theory's main strength is also its weakness, however. For, by focusing on ideological forms, it has been accused of underestimating the significance of structural class oppression. Critical theory has also been criticised for its pessimism regarding the possibilities for emancipatory change; its pseudoscientific methods, particularly in reference to psychoanalysis, and its 'ivory tower', academic detachment from reality. Critical theory has never crossed the border from theory to practice. It remains the privileged domain of middle-class university academics. As such, it has had little success in mobilising people against oppression (Jay 1996).

The edited volume *Critical Theory for Library and Information Science* (Leckie, Given, and Buschman 2010) exhibits these shortcomings. On one hand, its contributions succeed in showing how various ideologies and cultures maintain various forms of oppression in libraries. On the other hand, the volume's chapters neglect the role of material structures in maintaining these ideologies. There is also no core argument or strategy. The contributors draw on a range of conflicting traditions, including Western Marxism (Gramsci, Negri), fascism (Heidegger), social democracy (Giddens), psychoanalysis (Freud, Lacan) and post-structuralism (Barthez, Foucault), amongst others. Those drawing on psychoanalysis (Freud and Lacan) are pseudoscientific and therefore difficult to verify empirically. Predictably, the contributors tend to focus on offering criticisms rather than practical solutions. As such, the volume offers limited guidance for the public librarian looking for a clear and coherent strategy for combatting oppressive ideologies and practices.

Marxism-Leninism has always recognised the power of ideology in sustaining oppression. Unlike critical theory, however, it does not succumb to idealism by elevating ideology above the economic base, above the class system. It also constitutes a single, coherent body of theory, one based on a wealth of historical experience, and which offers clear, workable solutions. By adhering to Marxism-Leninism, this book recognises that the oppressive ideologies within public libraries are shaped and determined by their underlying material structures and practices. It is these structures that need changing above all else. This book outlines a clear and well-tested strategy for achieving this.

Western Marxism

It has been shown that Marxism is a broad church with many conflicting schools within it. In the field of library science, as in all the other academic disciplines, the doctrine known as 'Western Marxism' is the hegemonic variant. Western Marxism is less a definite position than it is an eclectic series of theories and methods. There are, however, some general tenets that all Western Marxists share. The most important one is that the fundamental theses of Marx and Engels have been invalidated by history and that they therefore need replacing in light of that fact. Western Marxists reject the basic ideas established by the classics of Marxism, and they have replaced them with several others, which are supposedly more useful for studying the modern-day Western nations (Anderson 1976). The main principles are as follows:

1. The denial that natural and social processes are law-governed: dialectical materialism cannot identify laws in the social world (since they do not exist), and it should instead function as a general heuristic to highlight its interconnectedness.
2. The 'retreat from class': the rejection of class as the core concept of Marxist analysis on the basis that a focus on class is necessarily reductionist or, in other words, too narrow and exclusive.
3. The rejection of the working class as the universal class that will bring about socialism: this principle is based on the view that the working class in the West has dissolved in light of de-industrialisation.

4 The rejection of the dictatorship of the proletariat: the redefining of socialism as a reformed liberal democracy, often called 'democratic socialism'
5 The view that Marxism-Leninism violates Marxism and that the socialist countries are totalitarian 'Stalinist' regimes that have long abandoned Marxism and socialism
6 The denial that Marxism is a science or, in other words, the denial that capitalism will collapse according to its own economic laws and that communism is the inevitable end point of social development
7 The augmenting of Marxism with bourgeois concepts and methodologies. It is here that Western Marxism overlaps with critical theory and intersectionality.
8 The detachment of Marxist theory from the class struggle: the transformation of Marxism from a revolutionary theory into a critical academic discipline

The 'Marxist' literature on libraries exhibits these characteristics. In *The Dialectic of Academic Librarianship: A Critical Approach*, Bales criticises the liberal excesses of the 'modern capitalist academic library' (MCAL; Bales 2015: 23). He rejects the uncritical association of the MCAL with 'Big-T Truth' ideals, such as democracy, equity, diversity and intellectual freedom. He presents the MCAL as an elitist institution, one that reflects the interests and power of the bourgeoisie. Popowich (2019) makes essentially the same argument in his book *Confronting the Democratic Discourse of Librarianship: A Marxist Approach*, although he broadens the scope of analysis beyond academic libraries to the other kinds.

The Western Marxist assumptions of these studies are worth highlighting. First, they briefly dismiss the Marxist-Leninist library systems as 'Stalinist' and 'state capitalist'. In agreement with the bourgeois critics of socialist libraries, they claim that these systems repressed the cherished principles of free thought and anti-censorship.

Second, they reject the significance of class in examining libraries. The concept is virtually absent in Bales's book, which relies mostly on dialectical materialism. Likewise, Popowich is more interested in highlighting the importance of gender, race and other non-class forms of oppression in libraries. As McNichol (2020: 69–70) explains in his review, 'Popowich's work falls squarely within the realm of "critlib"'. This is 'less a group than a position (or a series of interrelated positions) that queries how libraries and archives, as institutions, are "implicated in structures of domination organized around class, race, gender, sexuality, disability, etc."'. It is similar, in other words, to intersectionality.

Third, both authors identify the public library's mission with the support of a 'true' classless democracy rather than the working class. In the case of Bales, this approach has opened his argument to the charge of hypocrisy:

> Bales himself appears to fall into a non-dialectical, objective idealist trap of his own making, when in chapter seven he promotes dialectical librarianship as a path towards "progress" as well as "equality and freedom" (pp. 153–4): three very "Big-T Truths" offered without dialectical qualifications of any kind.
>
> (Dudley 2016: 110)

Fourth, both studies utilise a range of non-Marxist sources in developing their argument. Bales draws on liberal sociologists Max Weber and Karl Mannheim (Dudley 2016: 107), whilst Popowich draws on the utopian socialist Frederick Jameson, amongst others. Their assumption is that the concepts established by Marx and Engels cannot facilitate an adequate understanding of libraries.

Finally, Bales and Popowich detach Marxist library theory from practice. They do this by focusing mainly on criticisms and by drawing primarily on the academic literature. As Dudley (2016: 110) argues in reference to Bales's book, 'the concluding two chapters are rather disappointing and get us no nearer to moving beyond critique'. Likewise, McNichol (2020: 70) claims that Popowich's book 'is not a practical guide' but 'more of a theoretical discussion of potentially disruptive ways of existing prior to the revolution'. These characteristics place them firmly in the Western Marxist tradition.

This book provides an original contribution to the Marxist scholarship on libraries. For starters, it is the first to focus exclusively on public libraries. The rationale for this decision is that public libraries are distinct forms of organisation that cannot be lumped together with the other kinds. Only a dedicated examination can do them justice.

Second, this book repudiates Western Marxism in favour of a Marxist-Leninist analysis of public libraries. Whereas the current studies disregard Marxism-Leninism, this book defends its rich insights and its contemporary vitality. In doing so, it provides an original analysis of how Marxism-Leninism has been applied to the theory and practice of public libraries.

Third, this book places class at the centre of its analysis. This focus is not arbitrary. It is a basic principle of Marxism-Leninism, which demands a thorough class analysis of social phenomena. The public library cannot be understood without highlighting its class essence and function.

Fourth, this book assumes that the concepts and categories outlined by Marx and Engels, and developed by Lenin, are sufficient in providing a comprehensive understanding of public libraries. Indeed, the inclusion of non-Marxist ideas and concepts will only reduce the power of the Marxist analysis.

Finally, this book provides the first practical Marxist guide to action, by offering both criticisms and solutions. In doing so, it draws on the innovative work of library practitioners as well as academics. It takes seriously the Marxist thesis that theory and practice must inform each other. From beginning to end, this book is designed as a manual for not only understanding public libraries but transforming them too.

Structure

Having situated this book in relation to the critical scholarship on libraries, it is now time to outline its structure. For the Marxist, the fundamental task of social scientific research is to penetrate the surface forms of phenomena and expose their underlying essence. That is the aim of Chapter 2, which outlines the Marxist-Leninist interpretation of the public library. Marxism-Leninism reveals the essential class content of the concept, and it examines how this determines the forms of public library governance. Marxism-Leninism shows what power-exercising principles and methods, and in what forms of institutions and organisations, this essential class content is expressed.

The remaining chapters explore the Marxist-Leninist programmes for transforming public libraries. It does so in order to identify the key principles for building a working-class library. Marxism-Leninism is not a dogma, however, but a guide to action. Its ideas require adaptation to the changing environment and conditions. Because of this, the various socialist states established unique library systems for their own countries. Each has had different characteristics. Bearing that in mind, this book does not provide a survey of every socialist library system. Limitations of space have forced it to be selective in its selection of case studies and theorists. It does, however, claim to offer comprehensive coverage of the main Marxist-Leninist ideas on the phenomenon.

Chapter 3 examines the theory and practice of socialist public libraries in the Soviet Union, the world's first socialist state. The programmes and methods of public library organisation in the USSR were spelt out, and the experiences generalised, in Lenin's works and in the various documents of the Soviet state. All the problems that were encountered and reckoned with in public library construction in the other socialist countries, as well as the possible ways to their solution, were given detailed discussion in these writings. That is why the analysis of Soviet libraries draws mainly from them. Lenin's works are rich in theoretical content, and furthermore, they represent standpoints that became widely accepted in the communist movement. They serve as the theoretical basis for every Marxist-Leninist library programme. Consequently, these works have not ceased to be factors in contemporary socialist libraries.

Of all the countries based on Marxism-Leninism, North Korea's public library system has been the most distinct. Despite this, however, outside observers know the least about it. That is why Chapter 4 examines this secretive, misunderstood system, which is based on the *Juche* idea. It focuses mainly on the pronouncements of Kim Il-Sung, the founder of North Korea and its ruling party, the Workers Party of Korea. Kim's pronouncements became the law in the Democratic People's Republic of Korea (DPRK), and so his ideas provide some unique insights into the system as it functions today.

Although the Marxist-Leninist public library has developed the most in the socialist countries, it has also been realised, albeit to a lesser extent, in the capitalist countries too. Chapter 5 outlines the strategies and organisational principles for building this *Vanguard* library. It is called a 'Vanguard' library because of its specific class composition and purpose: it is a working-class organisation armed with Marxist-Leninist theory, and it aims to construct a library for the working class. Drawing on the insights of the Soviet Union and the DPRK, as well as other examples from the capitalist and socialist worlds, this chapter outlines some practical proposals for establishing these Vanguard libraries. It suggests how public librarians anywhere can strive to change their ideals, services and practices so that they can best serve the needs of the diverse working class, particularly as both this class and society evolve.

References

Anderson, P. (1976) *Considerations on Western Marxism*. Bristol: New Left Books.

Anghelescu, H. (2001) 'Romanian Libraries Recover after the Cold War: The Communist Legacy and the Road Ahead', *Libraries & Culture*, 36/1: 233–252.

Bales, S. (2015) *The Dialectic of Academic Librarianship: A Critical Approach*. Sacramento: Library Juice Press.

Benton, S. (2020) 'ULC President & CEO Issues Statement on the Role of Libraries in Dismantling Systemic Racism', *Urban Libraries Council* [online]. www.urbanlibraries.org/newsroom/ulc-president-ceo-issues-statement-on-the-role-of-libraries-in-dismantling-systemic-racism

Brown, J., Ferretti, J., Leung, S. and Mendez-Brady, M. (2018) 'We Here: Speaking the Truth', *Library Trends*, 67/1: 163–181.

Chou, L. and Pho, A. (eds.) (2018) *Pushing the Margins: Women of Colour and Intersectionality in LIS*. Sacramento: Library Juice Press.

Claeys, G. (2018) *Marx and Marxism*. London: Pelican.

Dudley, M. Q. (2016) 'Review of the Dialectics of Academic Librarianship: A Critical Approach', *Canadian Journal of Academic Librarianship*, 1/1: 107–110.

Edwards, E. (1859) *Memoirs of Libraries*. London: Trübner & Co.

——— (1864) *Libraries and the Founders of Libraries*. London: Trübner & Co.

Eisenstein, H. (2018) 'Querying Intersectionality', *Science & Society*, 82/2: 248–261.
GOV (n.d.) 'Libraries Deliver: Ambition for Public Libraries in England 2016 to 2021', *Gov.uk* [online]. www.gov.uk/government/publications/libraries-deliver-ambition-for-public-libraries-in-england-2016-to-2021/libraries-deliver-ambition-for-public-libraries-in-england-2016-to-2021
Guess, R. (1991) *The Idea of a Critical Theory: Habermas and the Frankfurt School*. Cambridge: Cambridge University Press.
Harris, G. and Creamer, R. (1996) *Better Read Than Dead: Libraries in Cuba, China, North Korea and Vietnam*. Link/ISC Conference Proceedings 16th March 1996, VSO, Putney, London, UK, Special Issue of "Link-Up", Vol. 8, No. 1.
Held, D. (2004) *Introduction to Critical Theory: Horkheimer to Habermas*. Cambridge: Polity Press.
Jay, M. (1996) *The Dialectical Imagination: A History of the Frankfurt School and the Institute of Social Research, 1923–1950*. Berkeley: University of California Press.
Kase, F. (1961) 'Public Libraries in Czechoslovakia under the Unified Library System', *The Library Quarterly*, 31/2: 154–165.
Kolakowski, L. (2005) *Main Currents of Marxism: The Founders, the Golden Age, the Breakdown*. New York: W. W. Norton and Company.
Kosciejew, M. (2009a) 'Inside an Axis of Evil Library: A First-Hand Account of the North Korea Dear Leader's Library System Part One', *Feliciter*, 55/4: 167–170.
——— (2009b) 'Inside an Axis of Evil Library: A First-Hand Account of the North Korea Dear Leader's Library System Part Two', *Feliciter*, 55/5: 207–209.
Kranich, N. (2001) *Libraries and Democracy: The Cornerstones of Liberty*. Chicago: American Library Association.
Kuusinen, O. (1961) *Fundamentals of Marxism-Leninism*. London: Lawrence and Wishart.
Leckie, G., Given, L. and Buschman, E. (eds.) (2010) *Critical Theory for Library and Information Science: Exploring the Social from across the Discipline*. Santa Barbara: Libraries Unlimited.
Lew, S. and Yousefi, B. (eds.) (2017) *Feminists among Us: Resistance and Advocacy in Library Leadership*. Sacramento: Library Juice Press.
McGarvey, D. (2017) *Poverty Safari: Understanding the Anger of Britain's Underclass*. Edinburgh: Luath Press.
McNichol, M. (2020) 'Review of the Book Confronting the Democratic Discourse of Librarianship: A Marxist Analysis by S. Popowich', *Pathfinder: A Canadian Journal for Information Science Students and Early Career Professionals*, 1/2: 68–71.
Mostecky, V. (1956) 'The Library under Communism: Czechoslovak Libraries from 1948 to 1954', *The Library Quarterly*, 26/2: 105–117.
Murison, W. (1988) *The Public Library: Its Origins, Purpose and Significance*. London: Clive Bingley.
Pateman, J. (2019) 'Lenin without Dogmatism', *Studies in Eastern European Thought*, 71: 99–117.

Popowich, S. (2019) *Confronting the Democratic Discourse of Librarianship: A Marxist Approach.* Sacramento: Library Juice Press.

Rubin, R. (2010) *Foundations of Library and Information Science*, 3rd ed. New York: Neal-Schuman Publishers.

Schlesselman-Tarango, G. (ed.) (2017) *Topographies of Whiteness: Mapping Whiteness in Library and Information Science.* Sacramento: Library Juice Press.

Şerbănuţă, C. (2017) 'Public Librarianship in Communist Romania: Creating a Profession to Serve the Socialist Propaganda Cause', *Library Trends*, 65/4: 615–638.

Sroka, M. (2013) 'Soldiers of the Cultural Revolution: The Stalinization of Libraries and Librarians in Poland, 1945–1953', *Library History*, 16/2: 105–125.

2 The Marxist interpretation of the public library

Introduction

The aim of this book is to outline the major Marxist views of public libraries and to then use these views as inspiration to propose a public library service for the working class. In order to achieve this aim, it is, first, important to understand the phenomenon being examined. For although the Marxists studied here have approached public libraries in various ways, they each share the same core interpretation of what it is. The aim of this chapter is to outline this shared interpretation. It identifies the fundamental assumptions and concepts that inform the Marxist public library theories outlined in this book.

In order to achieve that objective, the first section defines the concept of the public library. The second part explains the Marxist view that the public library is a cultural category. It then explores the relationship between the public library, on one hand, and democracy, equality and freedom, on the other. The final section discusses the notion that the public librarian is a historical phenomenon.

The concept of the public library

The foundation for the Marxist conception of the public library is contained in Lenin's 1913 article *What Can be Done for Public Education*. This compared the Western countries, which had public libraries, to Tsarist Russia, which had none. The tone of the piece is sarcastic and satirical. Although Lenin appears to oppose the notion of public libraries, he is actually endorsing them. 'There are quite a number of rotten prejudices current in the Western countries of which Holy Mother Russia is free', he writes:

> They assume there . . . that huge public libraries containing hundreds of thousands and millions of volumes, should certainly not be reserved only for the handful of scholars or would-be scholars that uses them.

Over there they have set themselves the strange, incomprehensible and barbaric aim of making these gigantic, boundless libraries available, not to a guild of scholars, professors and other such specialists, but to the masses, to the crowd, to the mob!

(Lenin 1983: 29)

This definition, although in an abstract form, that is not yet referring to the concrete points, expresses what the public library is *in general*. First, as a *library*, it is an information provider. It stores, organises, maintains and makes accessible informational material. Second, as a *public* service, its resources are not restricted to an exclusive minority. They extend 'to the masses, to the crowd, to the mob'. A public library signifies, at least formally, that everyone, including the 'hoi polloi', has the right to use its services. This is the basic, most bare-bones meaning of the term.

For the Marxist, however, things are not as simple as this. For 'although by rights' the public library 'is open to all', 'to give a right is one thing, to provide the possibility to enjoy that right is another' (Dobler 1983: 63). It is important, in other words, to distinguish between the public library in *theory* and the public library in *reality*. The latter must be situated within the economic structure of society and its social relations. Only then can one understand the essence of the public library as it exists in real life and not on paper. Only then can one obtain a scientific understanding of this phenomenon.

It is a fundamental Marxist thesis that the history of society is the history of class struggle. From ancient times onwards, the ruling class established institutions and services to help maintain their rule. The state, the legal system, the army, the police – all these coercive organs arose in order to control the oppressed in more or less explicit ways. The public library *was and is* one of these institutions. It is an instrument of the ruling, property-owning class. It is a power organ whose main function is to perpetuate the prevailing system of social relations. In class societies, the public library will never be 'neutral' or 'apolitical'. It will never serve everyone equally. As the Bolshevik library theorist F. Dobler expressed it,

is the big library open to all actually one for all the people? No, it is definitely dominated by one class of society, to be precise, the class on which the state system rests. . . . A library open to all . . . is definitely a class organisation.

(1983: 63)

A Marxist historical overview of the phenomenon can make this evident.

The first public libraries emerged in the ancient civilisations of Greece, Egypt and Rome. During this epoch, public services were uncommon. Since books were prized commodities, libraries were usually acquired through war or else purchased at great expense. This meant that public libraries were established mainly by the ruling class, which consisted of kings, military leaders, high-ranking statesmen and religious hierarchs. Although these libraries were nominally open to the public, the ancient understanding of the 'public' was very exclusive. It excluded women, who were limited to the private sphere, as well as the army of slaves whose labour ensured the maintenance of the ancient economy. To add to this, the supposedly 'free' toiling masses were illiterate and too downtrodden to use the libraries (Too 2010: 222). In practice, therefore, ancient public libraries served a tiny propertied male ruling class, which composed a minuscule portion of the population. They were propaganda instruments, containing mostly political documents and the official statements of this class (Woolf 2013: 6, 20). Since they were often some of the largest, grandest buildings in the area, usually situated within central government districts, their imposing physical presence reminded the masses of who ruled, and the masses themselves could never make effective use of the public libraries themselves. In short, they embodied the power, privilege and wealth of the ruling class.

With the rise of feudalism, public libraries grew in size and number. Like their ancient counterparts, these libraries catered to the ruling minority, which consisted of feudal lords, vassals, priests and the nobility. They excluded the exploited serfs and peasants, who remained illiterate and too oppressed to use them anyway. Little surprise then that the masses of ancient and feudal times did not view the public libraries as a means of enlightening themselves.

With the rise of capitalism, two main classes emerged: the proletariat and the ruling bourgeoisie. The former became an increasingly dangerous force to the latter. Unlike their predecessors in ancient times, a greater portion of the workers were literate and reading subversive literature disseminated by socialist and communist radicals. In response to this growing threat, bourgeois reformers promoted public libraries with the aim of safeguarding their class power, just like the ancient kings and feudal lords did before them. The need for these libraries became so great that the capitalist state intervened in the matter and became the leading force in establishing public libraries. These, in turn, became state institutions. The *Traditional* capitalist public library was born.

One of the earliest examinations of Traditional libraries can be found in Engels's 1844 work, *The Condition of the Working-Class in England*. Here, Marx's close collaborator examined the bourgeoisie's mechanics' institutes, which were forerunners to the nation's state-run public libraries. These provided adult education, particularly in technical subjects, to workers. Industrialists funded them on the grounds that they would benefit economically from having more knowledgeable and skilled employees. Another function was to provide the workers with an alternative pastime to gambling and drinking in pubs. The mechanics' institutes were designed to quell radical ideas spreading amongst the workers and keep them docile and obedient:

> Here the natural sciences are now taught, which may draw the working-men away from the opposition to the bourgeoisie, and perhaps place in their hands the means of making inventions which bring in money for the bourgeoisie; while for the working-man the acquaintance with the natural sciences is utterly useless *now* when it too often happens that he never gets the slightest glimpse of Nature in his large town with his long working-hours. Here Political Economy is preached, whose idol is free competition, and whose sum and substance for the working-man is this, that he cannot do anything more rational than resign himself to starvation. Here all education is tame, flabby, subservient to the ruling politics and religion, so that for the working-man it is merely a constant sermon upon quiet obedience, passivity, and resignation to his fate.
> (Engels 1975: 527)

Engels noted that the mechanics' institutes prohibited socialist publications and housed only those reading materials that engendered servility amongst the workers:

> [T]hat he [the industrialist] tolerates in the reading-room such prints only as represent the interests of the bourgeoisie, that he dismisses his employees if they read Chartist or Socialist papers or books, this is all concealed from you. You see an easy, patriarchal relation, you see the life of the overlookers, you see what the bourgeoisie promises the workers if they become its slaves, mentally and morally.
> (1975: 477)

The Traditional libraries served the same function as the mechanics' institutes. On one hand, they were institutions of *class control*. Bourgeois reformers saw them as a way of controlling and pacifying the working masses. By stopping the workers from turning to drink, irrational recreation and intellectual idleness, they would help prevent the spread of radical ideas. The bourgeoisie hoped that the sober literature provided in the public libraries would draw the workers away from the subversive socialist literature, which was revolutionary and harmful to their class dominance (Black 2000: 5).

Traditional public libraries were some of the 'ameliorative measures' taken to relieve pressure off the capitalist system when tensions mounted and there was concern about civil disobedience. It is no coincidence, for example, that the main roads leading to many municipal parks and public squares led straight to the local barracks so that troops could be despatched quickly to quell civil disorder. Traditional public libraries played the dual function of corralling and controlling working-class people during their idle time and steering them away from other less desirable pursuits (Corrigan and Gillespie 1978: 3).

Engels saw right through the bourgeoisie's attempt to 'buy the proletariat' with its Traditional public libraries. Although 'all the meetings and assemblies held for these objects resound with the praises of the workers', the bourgeoisie's aim, he correctly noted, was to mould an army of 'worthy, modest, useful' wage slaves, who could help improve profits (Engels 1982: 281). In 1851, a year after England passed the 1850 Public Libraries Act, Engels wrote to Marx discussing the bourgeoisie's plan to build a free library in Salford. He was confident that the workers would not be fooled by this act of benevolence. Engels was 'looking forward to the [bourgeoisie's] outburst of indignation at the ingratitude of the workers', which would inevitably 'break loose' (1982: 281). An indeed it did. The working class rejected these Traditional libraries, which they rightly recognised as being opposed to their interests (Corrigan and Gillespie 1978: 3).

The Traditional libraries of rising capitalism not only functioned as institutions of class control. As in ancient and feudal times, they also functioned primarily as institutions of *class exclusion*. In England, as in America, they were promoted primarily by the middle classes *for themselves*. They hoped that the libraries would function as research centres for the educated. For instance, they could enable manufacturers to improve their products and help teachers stay up to date with recent developments. 'Public libraries played a part in strengthening the class formation and consciousness of a middle-class seeking liberal change in the realms of production and politics' (Black 2000: 6). They provided a public space in which to challenge the authority of the landed aristocracy. The middle classes hoped to exclude the working classes from the public libraries, which they wanted solely for themselves. This was reflected in the disproportionally high numbers of middle-class users. As Dobler observed in his 1921 article,

> [i]t is . . . difficult for the worker and the poor in the broad sense of the word to master books in a public library in the same manner as they are used by the intellectuals and the bourgeoisie. As a result the library is dominated not by those who need books the most, who are to a lesser degree armed with knowledge and education and are therefore weaker in the struggle of life, but by those who since childhood have been used to books and accustomed to us[ing] them at every step. For the worker and the little-educated worker the library open to all is an

alien institution. Everything in that library bears and cannot fail to bear the imprint of the bourgeois reader who dominates it. It is according to his tastes that the books are selected, it is according to his conception that everything is arranged. The worker, unless he is highly qualified or developed, feels himself a stranger in that library.

(1983: 63–64)[1]

The exclusive character of Traditional bourgeois libraries continued into the inter-war years, when the growing white-collar middle-class workforce dominated the libraries. In the economic depression of the 1930s, they found the free services particularly useful. As for the working class, many of them became alienated from public libraries, in which they were deliberately made to feel uncomfortable and unwelcome. They rightly recognised that public libraries did not cater to them. After the Second World War, the Traditional public library continued to be fuelled by the growing welfare state. They catered increasingly to middle-class tastes and demands so that by the 1970s, 'the public library had in a sense reverted to type. It had assumed an unmistakable middle-class status in keeping with its historic image as an institution of highbrow culture and social refinement' (Black 2000: 7). The Traditional library had abandoned all pretence of being an alternative source of education and literacy for the working class – as envisioned by Carnegie and Dewey – and became in effect a taxpayer-subsidised bourgeois reading club. Public library collections were now dominated by hardback fiction as the middle-class patrons clamoured for the latest novels. Ironically, one of the objections to the early public libraries was that they should not provide 'fiction on the rates'.

Under capitalism then, the Traditional public library does not enlighten and empower the working masses. It instead excludes and pacifies the masses. In this respect, it performs the same function as the ancient and feudal public libraries.

The socialist revolution terminates this false public library that, although appearing in the form of a public service, actually means an exclusive service. The socialist transformation ensures the real rule of the oppressed masses and their extensive participation in the life and organisation of the public library. The Traditional library of capitalism is destroyed and replaced with the Community-Led library of socialism. What is more, this service becomes enshrined as a permanent, inviolable, irrevocable state policy for the first time in history. The socialist state devotes an unprecedented number of resources to their growth and improvement. Cutbacks to public library services, which occur periodically in capitalist countries, are abolished for good. The Community-Led library becomes a leading force in developing the cultural, political, economic and political powers of the ruling working masses.

26 The Marxist interpretation

This process, however, does not take place by simply extending public library services to people debarred from them earlier. The Community-Led libraries of the socialist revolution also break the opposition of the exploiting classes who are in the way of the socialist transformation. These classes may attempt to make use of the opportunities provided by the new public libraries in the interest of their opposition. These manipulations are facilitated by the fact that, on one hand, these elements have traditionally developed a great influence and, on the other, that in the course of the socialist transformation, several temporary difficulties arise. For example, among the working people, some wavering may appear. Making use of this, the exploiting classes might use the public libraries to influence the population very effectively, and this might endanger the construction of socialism. This is why from the capitalist Traditional library – which is inevitably narrow and stealthily pushes aside the poor and is therefore hypocritical and false through and through – forward development does not proceed simply, directly and smoothly towards progressively more public libraries. No. Simultaneously with this immense expansion, which creates a service for the poor, the people, the socialist Community-Led library imposes a series of restrictions on the services and resources that promote bourgeois ideas and undermine socialism.

It is only under communism that truly public libraries can exist. It is only in a communist society, where the resistance of the exploiting class has been completely crushed, when the middle class has disappeared, when there are no classes, that a truly *Needs-Based* public library can become possible and realised: a public library without any exceptions, restrictions or contradictions whatsoever, a public library that serves the diverse needs of every person who uses it. And only then will the class character of public libraries wither, owing to the simple fact that, freed from capitalist slavery, from the untold horrors, savagery, absurdities and infamies of capitalist exploitation, people will gradually become accustomed to seeing each other as equals. They will become accustomed to organising the public libraries without discrimination, without exclusion, without petty restrictions, without the special apparatus for class rule called the state.

This historical survey makes it evident that the public library does not automatically mean information and education for the majority of the population, that is the working people. And that is why, amongst other things, Marxism generally differentiates between three types, or, more precisely, three phases, in the development of the public library. The first type is the *Traditional library* existing in the exploiting societies. This type caters primarily to the ruling and middle classes and a small portion of the exploited. Here, the public character of the library is realised only exceptionally but never completely. The second type, or phase of development of the public library, is the *Community-Led library* practised during the transition from an exploiting society to communism. This is a public library for the poor, for nine-tenths of the population. It suppresses the services and information resources that serve to undermine socialism. This is almost a complete public library, with the only limitation being the suppression of capitalist influences. Finally, Marxism identifies the third type, or phase of development, of public library, namely that of the communist society. Here, there is a complete *Needs-Based library*, one that serves the entire population and has no limitations. It functions in accordance with the communist distributive principle 'from each according to their ability, to each according to their needs'.

Public libraries develop in accordance with the three laws of dialectical materialism. One of these is the law of the unity and conflict of opposites. This law appears in the conflict between the libraries' purpose, which is to serve the public, the working masses and the library's class essence, which causes it to discriminate against some groups. This contradiction drives the public library's development from a narrow, exclusive Traditional library into an inclusive Needs-Based library.

The second law of dialectical materialism is the transition of quantitative into qualitative change. This law appears in the public library's policies, which begin with small, incremental changes but which culminate in radical ruptures. For example, the Traditional library makes several piecemeal reforms before making a revolutionary change, which transforms it into a Community-Led library.

The third law of dialectical materialism is the negation of the negation. This law expresses the idea that each form of public library contains the seeds of the succeeding form within itself. The Traditional library contains the seeds of the Community-Led library, which, in turn, contains the seeds of the Needs-Based library. Each successive form also retains the progressive aspects of the old library whilst discarding the old, conservative aspects. For example, the Community-Led library retains the book stocks and technologies of the Traditional library whilst discarding its middle-class values.

As it becomes clear from this Marxist definition of the public library, in Marxism, there is no 'pure' public library, one independent of classes or definite social patterns. One *cannot speak of the public library in general*. It is only realistic to speak of the public library if one always describes the public library of what society, of what class and of what type. To repeat: there is no public library in general; there are only different public libraries defined by their class characteristics. Namely there are ancient, feudal, bourgeois (Traditional), socialist (Community-Led) and communist (Needs-Based) public libraries.

The public library as a cultural category

Marxism considers the public library to be a *cultural* category. Lenin 'judged the level of culture in a country by the way in which its libraries were run; he regarded the state of the libraries as an indication of the general level of culture' (Krupskaya 1957: 78). Likewise, Enver Hoxha, leader of the People's Socialist Republic of Albania, said that 'the development of the activity of libraries indicates the rise of the cultural level of the people' (1975: 46).

According to the Marxist *Dictionary of Philosophy*, culture, in its most general sense, denotes 'all the material and spiritual values created or being created by society in the course of history and characterizing the historical stage attained by society in its development'. It is customary to distinguish between *material* and *spiritual* culture. Material culture refers to the physical embodiments of the material wealth of a society. These include human creations like buildings and machines, as well as goods and instruments, broadly understood. Spiritual culture encompasses the behaviours and norms found in societies, as well as the knowledge, beliefs, arts, laws, customs and habits of the people in these societies. People acquire culture through the learning processes of enculturation and socialisation, which is shown by the diversity of cultures across and within societies. Culture always 'assumes a class character both as to its ideological content and its practical aims'. There is the culture of the ruling class, and there is the culture of the subjugated (Frolov 1984: 94).

Every class uses culture in their struggle to advance their interests and create a society that empowers them. It is often the public library that mediates, fixes and expresses in an institutional form the cultural relations between classes. It provides a good opportunity for the classes' cultural relationships to express themselves overtly, as it recognises, at least formally, the right of any social group to use its services and information resources. The public library, as a cultural category, also reflects the various classes' cultural levels. On one hand, it is a physical structure and therefore a form of material culture for a definite class. On the other hand, it is also an education provider and therefore a developer of spiritual culture for a definite class. The public library thereby indicates which classes have developed their culture – or at least certain aspects of it – and it also indicates which classes have not.

In class societies, the public library is an expression of the factual inequality of the social classes and strata. First, it expresses that a given class is ruling, which subordinates all the other social groups to its own interests. The public library also expresses that the ruling class has the dominant culture, which it utilises in its own interest. It not only debars other classes from using the library to develop their own culture. It also uses the library for imposing cultural restrictions on other classes and practising its class dictatorship over them. That is why the public library contributes to the domination of one portion of the population over the other. The public library does not and cannot change social inequality by acknowledging, on the cultural plane, the formal equality of people.

And yet the fact that in a capitalist republic, no less than in an ancient slave-owning state, the Traditional public library remains a tool for the oppression of one class by another by no means signifies that the form of library makes no difference to the exploited. In comparison to the ancient and feudal libraries, the capitalist Traditional library is a freer, more open, more inclusive form of library, one that can assist the workers in their struggle for cultural development.

But by acknowledging the right of the broad masses to develop their cultural levels and acquire knowledge, the public library is advantageous not only for the working masses. It is also an advantageous cultural form for the ruling class as well, particularly in exploiting societies. Indeed, the public library there provides an advantageous condition for maintaining the whole system of inequality in an undisturbed way. By recognising partial, formal, primarily legal-cultural equality, it conceals the social inequalities characteristic of the system. It arouses illusions about the system. Moreover, it also offers certain cultural forms of compensation for the most active elements of the lower classes. Its provision of books, information and learning resources has created cultural privileges and sops for the respectful, meek, reformist and patriotic office employees and workers, corresponding to their economic privileges and sops.

Since, according to historical materialism, culture is a part of the superstructure, the public library, as a cultural institution, functions in order to stabilise the economic base and, by extension, the rule of the property-owning class. The *Dictionary of Philosophy* makes this clear when it says that Marxism views the 'production of material goods as the basis and source' of culture. Nevertheless, it is also a key historical materialist thesis that the superstructure has a relative autonomy from the economic base, and this means that culture has some room to manoeuvre. 'It does not automatically follow changes in its material basis, being characterized by relative independence (continuity of development, reciprocal influence by the cultures of various peoples, etc.)' (Frolov 1984: 94). This means that the public library, as a part of this superstructure, need not always serve the dominant economic forces. Just like the whole of cultural life, the public library possesses relative autonomy.

Engels highlighted this point whilst examining the mid-nineteenth-century bourgeois mechanics institutes. At the same time highlighting their capitalist, Traditional essence, he also pointed out that the workers repudiated these institutions. Rather than abandon libraries altogether, however, they established their own 'proletarian reading-rooms' (Engels 1975: 527). Although these were established under capitalism, they did not serve the bourgeoisie. On the contrary, the working class established these libraries for themselves. They were, in other words, Community-Led and, to an extent, Needs-Based libraries:

> These different sections of working-men, often united, often separated, Trades Unionists, Chartists, and Socialists, have founded on their own hook numbers of . . . reading-rooms for the advancement of education . . . in the reading-rooms, proletarian journals and books alone, or almost alone, are to be found. . . . That . . . the working-men appreciate solid education when they can get it unmixed with the interested cant of the bourgeoisie, the frequent lectures upon scientific, aesthetic, and economic subjects prove which are delivered especially in the Socialist institutes, and very well attended . . .
>
> (Engels 1975: 527–528)

Engels (1975: 527) noted that the proletarian Community-Led and Needs-Based libraries were 'very dangerous for the bourgeoisie, which . . . succeeded in withdrawing several such institutes . . . from proletarian influences, and making them organs for the dissemination of the sciences useful to the bourgeoisie'. Indeed, despite their achievements in serving the working class, these libraries never became dominant. Since they lacked the financial backing of the capitalist state and bourgeoisie, they were less numerous and less prominent than Traditional libraries.

The resurgence of Community-Led and Needs-Based public libraries during the late twentieth century provides a more recent example of their relative autonomy. In the 1970s, class-conscious librarians became increasingly aware of the fact that Traditional public libraries catered primarily to the middle classes, and in response, they sought to promote them for the masses instead. The new ethos was that the public library should serve the masses, not the privileged minorities. It entailed a focusing of resources on the vulnerable and needy. Librarians were expected to conduct community work and not just organise books on the shelves. Needs-Based librarians took things a step further and sought to make libraries prioritise the marginalised groups in society.

The attempt to broaden and transform Traditional public libraries was met with stiff opposition by the bourgeoisie and capitalist state. The Community-Led and Needs-Based movement declined during the 1980s with the rise of neo-liberalism, which began an ideological offensive against all vaguely leftist ideas and practices. Within this climate, Traditional librarians increased in power and took up leading positions within the service. Although Community-Led and Needs-Based public libraries still exist today, the Traditional model remains dominant in the capitalist countries. This is because the Traditional public library is the optimal form for maintaining capitalism and the subjugation of the masses.

The significance of these historical examples is this: the public library is not a passive reflection of the economic base, one lacking in cultural autonomy or affectivity. Similar to the other cultural phenomena, it does react, in a relatively independent way, to the economic sphere of society. There are different class forces involved in the organisation of public libraries, and these forces participate in a constant struggle over libraries' organisation and purpose. This, in turn, gives libraries more opportunities to manoeuvre. In strained situations, for example, in a revolution or counter-revolution, these opportunities grow further and become more effective, or even perhaps dominating.

The public library may and does occasionally counterbalance the situational disadvantages of certain classes and social strata. It may and does modify such economic and other social circumstances that would otherwise remain unchanged. The public library may and does react back to the economy – depending on given laws and within the determined limits. This explains, for example, the fact that at the same economic development level, the various classes make efforts to realise different forms of public library, and the results of their activity lead to different utilisation of the libraries. Under capitalism, for instance, Community-Led and Needs-Based libraries have existed alongside the dominant Traditional libraries.

The public library, as a cultural phenomenon, may be one of the ways and means of achieving a certain economic result by a non-economic, cultural means. The public library may ensure a freer assertion of various interests and a freer struggle for them. It does not abolish class cultural oppression, but it does make the cultural struggle more direct, open and pronounced, which is what the exploited need.

The public library may help the exploited – who are in an economically subordinate position in the exploiting societies – in promoting the realisation of their interests through cultural means. The public library need not necessarily serve the ruling class and the dominant property relations. If this institution is established and controlled by the oppressed or its supporters, then it can serve the interests of these subjugated strata.

In exploiting societies, the public library and the struggle to broaden it not only constitute a field and means of striving to achieve better conditions, but – under definite circumstances – they may also be a means of surpassing the given conditions. The results of the struggle to broaden the public library gradually leads to the formulation, in workers' minds, of the necessity of realising socialism. As such, the more democratic the public library, the clearer will the workers see that the root evil is capitalism, not a lack of education or culture.

The struggle to broaden the public library forces open the frameworks of the existing system, it points beyond them, and in the case this programme is realised, it even surpasses them. Under capitalism, for instance, all public library services without exception are conditional, restricted, formal, narrow and difficult of full realisation. Yet no self-respecting Marxist will consider anyone opposing these rights a genuine socialist. Without the proclamation of these services, without a struggle to introduce them now, immediately, in an effort to develop the masses' cultural level, socialism will be impossible.

The struggle to broaden the public library under capitalism must be waged in a revolutionary and not a reformist manner. Struggles must go beyond the bounds of bourgeois legality, breaking them down, going beyond rants on internet blogs and verbal protests and drawing both the librarians and masses into decisive actions, extending and intensifying the struggle for every fundamental library demand up to a direct proletarian onslaught on the bourgeoisie, that is up to the socialist revolution that expropriates the bourgeoisie. Of course, this cultural struggle in itself does not realise the complete liberation of the proletariat, but it may and does create better conditions for the liberation struggle. A proletariat that has failed to raise their cultural level and knowledge via the public libraries is incapable of performing an economic revolution. Capitalism cannot be vanquished without taking over the banks and repealing private ownership of the means of production. These revolutionary measures, however, cannot be implemented without the entire population using the libraries to raise their cultural level and class consciousness. Likewise, victorious socialism will be unable to consolidate its victory and bring humanity to communism without fully broadening the public libraries and bringing culture to the entire people.

Naturally, the Traditional public libraries of exploiting societies do not primarily favour the exploited and oppressed classes. They actually enable the exploiting classes to exercise their power in a more effective way. In fact, the public library in the exploiting systems conceals the actual power relationships and turns workers' attention away from the main problems, namely the social ones. It is in this way that the public library can become an effective cultural cover for capitalism.

By involving the working masses, the public library in socialist societies makes it possible to accelerate the realisation of a new type of life, one that is in the interest of the majority. The involvement of the broad masses of workers in the life of the public library – which increases their cultural level, their class consciousness and activity – is both an achievement of and a precondition for the progress of socialism and communism.

As it turns out, from the preceding, the broadening of the public library is *not an end in itself* but a means to achieve an end surpassing it. The public library would be useless to the workers if they could not use it immediately to develop their cultural level, educate themselves and fulfil their needs. Likewise, under socialism, the public library is part of this important objective, and it also promotes its realisation. But it does not by itself fulfil this objective.

Consequently, the public library as a means (even under socialism) is always subordinated to the purpose, the objective, namely the effective construction of socialism and communism. It is in this context that Marxism evaluates the public library and the development of its services.

Since the public library is only a cultural phenomenon, the working class cannot rest satisfied with its full realisation. The proletariat must go beyond the cultural sphere and extend its revolutionary activity of transformation to all fields of society. In other words, cultural emancipation means only the partial liberation of the people. Formally, it declares people to be conscious beings. The task is to realise this conscious community. That is cultural emancipation must be extended to become social emancipation.

Indeed, the public library by itself cannot cure social ills. The poor cannot win a victory, cannot accomplish their struggle against the rich, for the complete elimination of social inequality via the public library alone, that is the cultural field.

The public library is of enormous importance to the working class in its struggle against the capitalists for its emancipation. But the public library is by no means a boundary not to be overstepped. It is only one of the means of struggling to overcome capitalism and build communism. The public library means mass culture. The significance of the proletariat's struggle for mass culture becomes clearer if it is interpreted as meaning the end of class cultural distinctions. But as soon as all members of society assume control over the state, the economy and the other spheres of society, humanity will be confronted with the question of advancing further, from mass power in culture to mass power in political, economic and social life.

From the fact that the public library is a cultural category, it also follows that the widely spread views, actually illusions, which consider the public library to be a kind of remedy capable of solving every problem, are unjustified. The public library by itself does not create any new material value. It does not lead to an abundance of products nor to welfare, and it does not make the people free and happy. The public library may, by raising the masses' cultural level, promote better decisions in the fields of the economy and politics and in the various areas of intellectual life; it may help in involving more and more people in the execution of the previously mentioned decisions; it may influence people to lead a more rational and effective life by making use of the opportunities offered by socialism. Consequently, it may promote a faster advance of society.

The public library is a cultural means, and understood as such, it has advantages and deficiencies. The working masses and librarians must be aware of this and take it into account when they estimate or realise the possibilities it provides or when they evaluate the results achieved by a public library service. In doing so, they must take care not to underestimate either the public library or the illusions that have developed in connection with it.

The public library, democracy, freedom, and equality

In bourgeois discourse, the public library is often equated with positive, widely supported ideals. The most common ones are democracy, freedom and equality. In the words of the Chartered Institute of Library and Information Professionals,

> [l]ibraries are places where democracy, freedom and equality are not only respected but celebrated. The unique added value of a library is that it makes these outcomes universally accessible and relevant on equal terms to all members of the community.
>
> (LGA 2017: 7)

This purported relationship has two aspects. On one hand, the public library is presented as the *embodiment* of these principles. It supposedly realises democracy, freedom and equality in its organisation and services. On the other hand, it is argued that public libraries support democracy, freedom and equality *within society at large*. A Marxist analysis of the social content of these concepts shows that neither of these claims is true.

The very presentation of this relationship is based on unscientific assumptions. Bourgeois scholars begin by imagining a public library 'in general', one lacking in class content, and they then portray it as a promoter and embodiment of 'pure' democracy, 'pure' freedom and 'pure' equality, each of which is also given neutral, above-class content. This presentation ignores the fact that each concept has a class essence, which, in turn, makes it misleading to talk about these concepts as pure categories. Indeed, they cannot be compared as such. The pure public library cannot be compared to pure democracy, freedom or equality, since none of these exists in reality. It is instead proper to compare the library of a particular class to the democracy, freedom or equality of a particular class. Once this is done, it becomes evident that their relationship is *not always positive*. An examination of these concepts can make this clearer.

Democracy

Democracy means the 'rule of the people'. In a democracy, every member of the community can have a say in governing their public affairs by participating in major political decisions. To be precise, it is the decisions of the majority that reign supreme in a democracy, and this majority is usually gauged through a vote or a show of hands. As such, democracy, as the rule of the people, is also the rule of the majority. This is what democracy means in general.

In class-divided societies, democracy, like the public library, is a class concept. It expresses the rule of a definite class. In exploiting societies, democracy exists for the exploiters, the minority, and it is denied to the exploited, the majority, who are squeezed out of politics. Under socialism, by contrast, democracy exists for the working-class majority, and it is denied to the exploiting minority.

The public library has no definite relation to political democracy, first, because public libraries have existed in undemocratic societies. For centuries, they existed in ancient and feudal societies where despotic and monarchical regimes dominated. A notable example was the Great Alexandrian Library established in ancient Egypt, under the Ptolemy dynasty. This library in no way encouraged the emergence of democracy there. It actually helped suppress the masses and cement the rule of Egypt's kings.

Democracies have also existed without public libraries. Several ancient Greek city-states were democratic, yet there is no surviving evidence that they all had public libraries. Even bourgeois democracy developed in places without public libraries for a long time. Finally, some democratic societies have also reduced their public libraries. This has happened recently in the United Kingdom. Upon the basis of bourgeois democracy, the British neo-liberal state has for several years now been cutting public library services.

Libraries can be a force for promoting democracy, but their precise class forms must be specified. Under bourgeois democracy, the Traditional library endorses democracy for the exploiters and dictatorship for the working class. Under socialism, the Community-Led library endorses democracy for the working class and dictatorship for the old exploiters and counter-revolutionaries. It is only under communism that the Needs-Based library endorses democracy for all.

The public library can be a force for promoting the further democratisation of society. It can promote the progression from despotism to communist democracy. However, it can only serve this function if it is a Community-Led or Needs-Based library. The Traditional libraries of the exploiting societies are a conservative force. They function in order to maintain the rule of the exploiters. They oppose the democratisation of society.

Public libraries do not necessarily embody democratic principles. The ancient, feudal, and Traditional bourgeois libraries are authoritarian in their internal organisational structure. The managers direct them from above, and the staff and patrons have minimal control over the life and development of the libraries. The socialist Community-Led library has a more democratic structure. In consultation with the library staff and masses, the workers' state formulates a plan for the library's general development. The staff and patrons also participate in the management, decisions and organisation of the library, albeit to varying degrees. Under communism, whereby the state has withered, the communist Needs-Based library has a fully democratic structure. The masses have complete control over its organisation and development. Every aspect of the library is controlled by them.

It follows from all this that there is no inherently positive relationship between the public library and democracy. This is a myth promoted by bourgeois ideologists.

Freedom

Marxism views freedom as an objective state of being, in which the individual has the resources to assert their positive actions and achieve their goals, free from external constraints. The achievement of complete freedom requires the full realisation of *human needs*. People will only be able to assert their positive actions and achieve their goals when all their human needs are met. Marxism places human needs in a hierarchy, which is helpful to visualise as a pyramid. At the bottom are the basic physiological needs of the human being – food, water, shelter and other essentials. People must meet these needs first before they can go about doing anything else. On the next level are safety needs, which people require to achieve security for themselves. These include personal, emotional and employment security, in addition to health and well-being. Next are the social needs. These are interpersonal and entail a feeling of belongingness. They require that people secure stable relationships with their friends, family and loved ones. Once people obtain this level, they can strive for their self-esteem needs. These concern one's ego and status. They involve people gaining recognition and respect from others. Finally, there is self-actualisation. This is a state of being in which the individual realises their full potential and can pursue whatever goals they want. In order to obtain self-actualisation, the individual must not only fulfil their lower-level needs but also master them. Self-actualisation is identical to freedom. A structural precondition for the realisation of this goal is the abolition of classes, since class oppression prevents some people from acting freely. Freedom also requires the creation of material abundance. It is only when society can produce a wealth of goods – both spiritual and material – that people will have the time and power to pursue their various creative activities. The abolition of classes and the creation of material abundance is achieved only under communism, a society that functions in accordance with the principle: 'from each according to their ability, to each according to their need'. As such, the realisation of freedom is a graudual, historical process.

The public library does not necessarily serve society-wide freedom, nor does it necessarily embody freedom. In antagonistic societies, the public library is an institution of class domination. It serves some classes whilst discriminating against others. It does not give everyone the same freedom to access its information and use its services. For some, primarily for the ruling classes, the public library supports and embodies freedom. For others, most notably the excluded classes, it is the enemy of freedom.

Ancient, feudal and Traditional bourgeois public libraries – by prioritising the provision of books and information – focus on the needs of the privileged whilst neglecting the needs of the oppressed. Far from promoting freedom, these libraries deny it to the subjugated classes. Socialist Community-Led libraries guarantee that the working masses can use their services. In doing so, they help all members of the community achieve their needs, particularly their higher-level ones. At the same time, they prohibit those policies and information resources that promote bourgeois ideas. Socialist libraries therefore promote the realisation of partial freedom. Communist Needs-Based libraries remove all service and resource limitations. They also help the masses fulfil not only their higher-level needs but their basic physiological and safety needs as well. Communist libraries therefore embody and support freedom.

Equality

Marxism separates equality into its narrow, formal dimension and its broader, human dimension. Formal equality is an immaterial state of being. It means that every person has an equal right to a particular good, and no one's right is stronger than anyone else's. Human equality, by contrast, is a *material* state of being. It exists when everyone is of the same economic status, social rank and power. Human equality does not mean that everyone has identical possessions. It does, however, mean that there are no *structural* disparities in economic and social power. Needless to say, this state of affairs requires and means the abolition of classes, for there can be no economic and social equality in a society in which one class oppresses another. Human equality is possible only under communism, a classless society lacking social distinctions, a society in which the popular masses control their economic affairs in common.

The public library may contradict formal equality. In the class societies, in which the public library prioritises some classes over others, it violates the principles of equal treatment and equal access. This is the case even under socialism, where the Community-Led libraries prioritise the working masses to the detriment of the exploiters. It is only in a classless communist society that the Needs-Based library grants everyone truly equal access to its services.

The public library may also contradict human equality. In an exploiting society riven by class antagonisms, it functions in order to maintain, or even widen, the social and economic inequality of the populace. Under capitalism, for instance, the Traditional public library helps educate, empower and enrich the middle-class, thereby increasing the economic and social inequality between them and the working class. Under socialism, the Community-Led library serves human equality by enriching the proletariat spiritually and materially. Even here, however, social and economic distinctions remain. The public library will serve the achievement of human equality only under communism. These communist Needs-Based libraries, by serving the specific needs of all, help prevent the emergence of structural economic and social disparities.

It follows, from this Marxist examination, that the public library cannot be automatically equated with the promotion of democracy, freedom or equality. Nor can the public library itself be automatically viewed as the embodiment of these ideals. When speaking of their relationship, it is necessary to speak of the public library of a definite class and democracy, freedom and equality for definite classes. This is the only way that their relationships can be correctly clarified.

The public librarian as a historical phenomenon

The public librarian is a professional who works in the public library. The job involves special training and a degree of knowledge that set librarians apart from the populace. In capitalist countries, it is generally supposed that public libraries cannot function without public librarians, without trained professionals. The mainstream view is that without the latter, the former would dissolve into anarchy and disorganisation. Running a public library requires a level of specialised knowledge and expertise that only educated professionals can provide, so the narrative goes.

Marxism rejects this view. It maintains that *there is no necessary connection between the public librarian, on one hand, and the public library, on the other*. This separation is based on historical facts. In ancient times, wealthy merchants, statesmen and other elites funded public libraries out of their own pockets and staffed many of them with untrained slaves and servants. These working people, who worked and organised the libraries, were not educated professionals. They did not undertake formal courses in library science. There was no standard higher education curriculum in librarianship in ancient times. No. The fact of the matter was that many of the public libraries were run and organised by slaves and other elements of the uneducated underclass. Since these people did not possess formal training, and since they were not trained specialists, they were not public librarians in the modern sense of the word.

With the rise of industrial capitalism in the nineteenth century, there were two major changes in the character of public librarians. One was that the working masses created their own, self-organised libraries for the first time in history. Engels showed that the proletarian reading rooms established during the mid-1800s were managed by the workers themselves and without professional librarians. So, too, were the miners' libraries in South Wales, which the miners established during the 1920s. These were more popular than public libraries in mining communities operated by professional librarians. However, these self-organised workers' libraries were successful mainly because their stocks and readerships were small and therefore easier to manage.

And this leads to the second change in public librarians during the rise of capitalism. In order to quell the rising working-class discontent and middle-class demands, the state replaced the private individual as the chief creator of public libraries. It began building them on a far greater scale, which led to a greater demand for public librarians. This growth of public libraries, in terms of both number and size, resulted in the theories, methods, procedures and forms of public library organisation becoming more complex and sophisticated. The public libraries began to develop new forms of cataloguing, management and organisation whilst also expanding their range of services. These changes made the old, untrained librarians unfit for the tasks of modern public librarianship. There was a greater need for trained, specialised librarians, who could utilise the most recent developments in technology and science to establish efficient public library systems. The higher education establishment met this demand. Universities and colleges created formal educational courses in library science, which were attended mostly by the middle classes. As a result, the untrained library staffs were gradually replaced by trained petit-bourgeois professionals. The class composition of librarians changed. As capitalism developed, middle-class personnel supplanted the working-class ones. The petit-bourgeois profession of public librarianship was thereby established, and it has grown ever since. To be a public librarian in many capitalist countries today, one has to take a library science course at university. In this sense, it is a middle-class professional occupation, just like being a doctor or lawyer.

Under socialism, as under capitalism, professional public library staffs remain necessary, since the average worker lacks the necessary knowledge to immediately organise the gigantic libraries effectively. Librarians are needed in order to manage the colossal books stocks, apply the most recent scientific methods of organisation and meet the masses' complex and constantly evolving demands. The main difference is that under socialism, unlike capitalism, the working class take up the majority of librarian posts whilst those with petit-bourgeois mentalities are thrown out. These staffs also help the worker patrons, rather than shun them, by answering their requests, offering assistance, assessing their needs and suggesting what resources to use. Although they act as humble servants of the workers, they still perform a distinct, specialised function, one that requires formal training.

This is not a permanent state of affairs, however. With the rapid development of technology, information technology and book and information stocks under socialism, the library functions become simplified over time. As this happens, the ordinary workers – who are better educated and more competent than ever – can perform more of the library administration tasks, and the trained professionals need to do less. In proportion, as society progresses towards communism, the public library profession gradually withers. The masses of workers will perform more of the library functions on a rotational, voluntary basis, and the historical distinction between the librarian and patron will diminish. Some of the now-extinct socialist countries went some way towards achieving this goal. In Ceausescu's Romania, for instance, 'library science education was discontinued in the mid-1970s on the assumption that anybody holding an undergraduate degree could perform as a librarian' (Anghelescu 2005: 441).

Under communism, the people will be of a high educational and cultural level. The productive forces will be able to provide a material abundance of books and information to the masses, and advanced technologies will simplify public library functions enough for all people to carry them out. This means that any citizen will be able to contribute to the daily administration, management and development of the public libraries. There will no longer be any need for a specially trained library staff, separated from the people. The libraries will become truly public, not only in the sense that they serve everyone but also in the sense that they are organised by everyone, the public. There will be no difference between librarians and patrons. Indeed, librarians as such will cease to exist. The profession will disappear.

The ahistorical, unscientific slogan 'public libraries need public librarians' is a petit-bourgeois slogan. The ideologists of capitalism promote it in order to perpetuate their elitist middle-class profession and keep it inaccessible to the working masses. The Marxist librarian fights to create a society not in which librarians are indispensable but in which there are no librarians, or, to express the same point in a different way, they fight to create a society in which everyone can be a public librarian.

Conclusion

The essence of the Marxist interpretation of the public library should have become clear from this chapter. Marxism shows that in order to take a scientific approach to the concept of the public library, it is necessary to detach the two sides of the concept, which are in close interdependence:

a   Who holds the power, or, more precisely, what class or classes does the public library serve; who is the master of the means of production in a given society? As a rule, the economic power and the library power are in the hands of the same social forces.
b   What is the way in which power is exercised, what is the form of the public library, how is the library managed and to what extent do the staff and patrons take part in its management. What services does the library provide?

These two elements are in organic connection, although the first of them has a decisive weight compared with the second as it represents the objective element that, ultimately, determines the class character of the public library and, by this, the actual limits of its achievement, both at the level of the library's cultural development and at that of the patron's cultural level.

The merit of Marxism consists in the fact that, by making a dialectical analysis of the public library, it does not give an absolute value to either side but appreciates them in their interdependence, granting to each one the true significance and part that it plays in the social process of developing the public library. The non-Marxist views, on the contrary, overlook the essential question of who holds the power and adopt as norms of appraising the public library the elements merely depending on the form of service or on the formal proclamation of the patron's equal right to use it.

Marxism takes into account the historical and class character of the public library in relation to the social and political order. Accordingly, on the grounds of historical facts, the Marxist view has reached the conclusion that an abstract public library or 'pure public library' does not exist. The public library is a cultural-historical category, the content of which changes from one order to another. The public library always has a class character, being directly linked to the nature of political power. The public library is determined by the essence of the social order and, in the final analysis, by the form of production relationships in the given society.

The true nature of the public library and its institutions is the result of the fight of the popular masses against social and cultural oppression. The fight for the public library is interwoven with the fight for progressive social changes.

The public library, as a form of culture, may express either the rule of the exploiting classes (all the exploiting societies) or the rule of the people (e.g. socialist democracy).

When the public library expresses the rule of the exploiting classes under bourgeois social conditions, the working class can also use it to further their cultural education, and they must make every effort to develop the public library in a way that the resulting situation may become an advantageous starting point for the socialist revolution.

The public library as a form of culture denotes a service for the people. Until it is fully realised it figures as a tool of struggle for proletarian education and emancipation. After the socialist revolution has achieved victory, it becomes a means in the hands of the people, of the workers, to be used in the interests of their social liberation. It becomes a public library for the workers, and it means continual interference, through state means too, in the public library in the interests of attaining socialism and communism.

This interpretation of the public library forms the theoretical basis for the Marxist library programmes outlined in the remainder of this book. It is now time to examine these programmes in more detail.

Note

1 Lenin himself read and commented on Dobler's article. In the margin next to this passage, he wrote, '[T]rue!' (Lenin 1983: 64).

References

Anghelescu, H. G. B. (2005) 'European Integration: Are Romanian Libraries Ready?', *Libraries & Culture*, 40/3: 435–454.

Black, A. (2000) 'Skeleton in the Cupboard: Social Class and the Public Library in Britain Through 150 Years', *Library History*, 16/1: 3–12.

Corrigan, P. and Gillespie, V. (1978) *Class Struggle, Social Literacy, and Idle Time: The Provision of Public Libraries in England*. Brighton: Noyce.

Dobler, F. (1983) 'The Modern Library System', in V. I. Lenin (ed.) *Lenin and Library Organisation*, pp. 62–65. Moscow: Progress Publishers.

Engels, F. (1975) *Marx Engels Collected Works*, Vol. 4. London: Lawrence and Wishart.

—— (1982) *Marx Engels Collected Works*, Vol. 38. London: Lawrence and Wishart.

Frolov, I. T. (eds.) (1984) *Dictionary of Philosophy*. Moscow: Progress Publishers.

Hoxha, E. (1975) *Selected Works*, Vol. 2. Tirana: 8 Nentori Publishing House.
Krupskaya, N. K. (1957) *On Education*. Moscow: Foreign Languages Publishing House.
LGA (Local Government Association) (2017) *Delivering Local Solutions for Public Library Services: A Guide for Councillors*. London: Local Government Administration.
Lenin, V. I. (1983) *Lenin and Library Organisation*. Moscow: Progress Publishers.
Too, Y. L. (2010) *The Idea of the Library in the Ancient World*. Oxford: Oxford University Press.
Woolf, G. (2013) 'Introduction: Approaching the Ancient Library', in J. Konig, K. Oikonomopoulou and G. Woolf (eds.) *Ancient Libraries*, pp. 1–22. Cambridge: Cambridge University Press.

3 V. I. Lenin and the Soviet socialist public library system

Introduction

The October Revolution of 1917 was a landmark event in the history of Marxism and public libraries. Under the leadership of V. I. Lenin, the Bolshevik Party seized power in Russia with the support of the fighting working class and began to construct the world's first socialist state (Pateman 2019b). A distinctive feature of the Bolshevik Party – which later became the Communist Party of the Soviet Union (CPSU) – is that it founded Marxism-Leninism and made it the sole *guide* for its activities. In doing so, the CPSU was able to lead the proletariat to victory in its struggle to overthrow capitalism. Following its example, several other workers' parties established socialist states in the twentieth century, and they all did so based on Marxism-Leninism. To this day, no other variant of Marxism has achieved political power. As such, only Marxism-Leninism has been able to establish socialist public libraries in practice.

During the course of building communism, the CPSU devoted significant attention to building a public library service for the masses. This provided the theoretical and organisational basis for services in the other Marxist-Leninist countries. It also provides some of the key principles of the Vanguard library, outlined in Chapter 5. That is why this chapter outlines the essential principles of the Soviet system.

The fundamentals of socialist public library organisation were established by none – other than Lenin himself. Besides being a revolutionary leader, he also showed intense interest in questions of culture, and as such, libraries were of central importance. The Bolshevik M. N. Pokrovsky, a leading figure in Soviet education, confirmed this during the First Library Congress of the Russian Soviet Federative Socialist Republic (RSFSR) in 1924:

> Precisely his concern for library organization, for spreading books, . . . for bringing books closer to the masses is what in the first place engraved itself in my memory, and I shall never be able to forget that. It was not

just a coincidence, but was due to the very nature of our revolution, and in this as in everything else Vladimir Ilyich was its most typical and brilliant mouthpiece.

(1983: 179)

The significance of this fact, as Dudley explains, is that 'heads of state with such personal and political interest in developing libraries [are] . . . rare' (1968: 8). They are rare indeed. It is no exaggeration to suggest that Lenin *led* the development of Soviet public libraries. He did not do so alone. Several other Bolsheviks contributed significantly, and it was the working class who did the hard work of building them. Nevertheless, Lenin was the guiding force. He set the general course of direction for public library construction, and he oversaw every major decision made regarding them. Lenin's works therefore provide the central focus of this chapter.

Lenin on the socialist public library

Lenin grew up in tsarist Russia, a repressive, quasi-feudalistic autocracy. It was founded on the exploitation of the proletariat and peasantry. The ruling class – which consisted of aristocrats and landowners – recognised that public education, by raising the cultural level of society, would encourage the masses to oppose their exploitation and the autocratic system. As such, the regime was 'totally unconcerned for public education'. In an effort to safeguard their rule, the landowners' government routinely repressed and opposed the development of public libraries. The few that did exist were of a Traditional stripe. They were funded by the ruling aristocracy and designed to pacify and exclude, rather than educate, the masses. Prior to the October Revolution, the public libraries had 6 books per 100 people, and the readership was below 3 million in a country with a population over 100 million (Chubaryan 1972: 68, 27).

Lenin had nothing but contempt for Russia's so-called people's libraries. 'Whenever you see a signboard: "People's Library" – you can afford to exult', he wrote sarcastically in 1913. 'There you will find cheap or even free pamphlets issued by the Union of the Russian People or the All-Russia Nationalist Club, under the medical supervision of the spiritual censorship'. These were reactionary monarchist organisations that sought to quell the revolutionary spirit of the fighting working class (Lenin 1983: 28). Lenin's wife, the Bolshevik revolutionary N. K. Krupskaya (1924), recalled that the 'people's libraries' 'were filled with moralizing discourses, religious booklets reflecting the viewpoint of the Black Hundred [a reactionary ultra-nationalist movement] – such as the anti-Semitic Visits of *Our Lady to the Tortures*, – monarchistic twaddle, and the like'.

In July 1913, Lenin wrote his seminal article 'What Can Be Done for Public Education'. In this work, he not only laid the foundation for the

Marxist interpretation of the public library. He also established the basic principles of the socialist public library. Lenin begins by establishing the class content of his vision. Under socialism, he argues, public libraries containing millions of volumes should not serve an exclusive minority. That is the bourgeois meaning of *public*. In a socialist society, a genuinely 'public' library should serve 'the masses, to the crowd, to the mob . . . the *Hoi Polloi*', in short, the *working class* (Lenin 1983: 29–30).

Having connected this class to the word *public*, Lenin goes on to identify the key metrics for gauging the development of a socialist public library. First, instead of creating bureaucratic regulations restricting book use, the libraries should ensure 'that even *children* can make use of the rich collections' and 'that readers can read publicly-owned books at home'. For socialists, 'the pride and glory of a public library' should not be 'the number of rarities it contains' but

> *the extent* to which books are distributed *among the people*, the number of new readers enrolled, the speed with which the demand for any book is met, the number of books issued to be read at home, the number of children attracted to reading and to the use of the library.

In other words, socialist public libraries should try to maximise the number of books read by the working masses. They are successful to the extent that they get working-class people into the library reading and taking out books (Lenin 1983: 29).

As Lenin recognises, however, it is often the case that 'only a few people can visit the library'. Due to their busy lifestyles or proximity, it may be too inconvenient for workers to visit them. As such, 'the rational organisation of educational work' should be 'measured by the number of books issued to be read at home, by the conveniences available to *the majority of the population*'. In the long term, a socialist society should have, at a minimum, 'a branch of the Public Library . . . within ten minutes' walk of the house of every inhabitant' (Lenin 1983: 30).

Lenin promotes the socialist public library as 'the centre of all kinds of institutions and establishments for public education'. Besides offering help to readers, they could provide 'a place for evening lectures, for public meetings and for rational entertainment'. These passages are significant. In contrast to bourgeois libraries, where the focus is on supplying information, Lenin envisions the socialist public library as a '*centre*' for social and cultural events. He deliberately refuses to specify what these events should be. He wants the socialist library service to be creative in what it delivers. It should provide any and all services that aid the working masses, and it should strive to become the best place to go for such services (Lenin 1983: 30).

Lenin adds that the public libraries should provide books in different languages so as to cater for all the major nationalities in the area. Besides this, they should institute a 'special, central, reading-room for children', and 'the librarians [must] do everything for the children's convenience and answer their questions'. This recommendation reflects Lenin's view that children are the future of socialism. If children go to the libraries and are treated with care and devotion, they will develop their educational and cultural levels from a young age and grow into ideal communist citizens (Lenin 1983: 30–31).

Lenin places public libraries at the heart of socialist culture and education. The bourgeois utopia of a dusty quiet library, where everyone sits in their own cubicle and the librarians only tend to their books, has no place in his socialist vision.

If the *Communist Manifesto* is the founding document of Marxian socialism, then 'What Can Be Done for Public Education' is the founding document of the Marxist socialist public library. When he published it in 1913, however, Lenin had to wait four more years until he could put these ideas into action. In January 1914, the tsarist state took more oppressive measures against the public libraries in its desperate attempt to quell the rumblings of the growing working-class movement. As Lenin observed at the time,

> [t]here are hardly any illiterates in the civilised countries. . . . Every thing is done to set up libraries. Over here, the Ministry of Public, what you might call, 'Education' resorts to the most desperate efforts, to the most ignominious police measures to hamper the cause of education and to prevent the people from acquiring knowledge! . . . apart from the persecution of the press in general, apart from the wild measures *against* libraries in general, rules which are a hundred times more restrictive are being issued *against* the public libraries! This is an outrageous policy of *benighting* the people, an outrageous policy of the landowners, who want the country to become *barbaric*.
>
> (1983: 31)

Through his personal experience with public libraries, Lenin learnt that they are class institutions which can serve the interests of either the exploited or the exploiters. This was an insight he never forgot during the construction of socialism in Soviet Russia.

The October Revolution and the tasks of Soviet public libraries

The October Socialist Revolution toppled the bourgeoisie and brought the working class into power. The workers gradually wrested the means of production from private hands and took them into collective ownership. They also dismantled the bureaucratic parliamentary apparatus and replaced it with their own proletarian democracy. By doing so, the working class ensured their political and economic domination.

The transition from socialism to communism required the development of technology and productive forces. This would gradually create a society of material abundance, diminish the distinction between mental and manual labour and eventually abolish classes themselves. This development, however, required a highly educated and cultured workforce, one able to comprehend and apply the latest discoveries in science and technology. The masses had to attain a high cultural level in order to carry out communist construction.

The major issue in Russia was that although the October Revolution carried out a *political* and *social* revolution, it did not carry out an *economic* or *cultural* revolution. It took place not in an advanced capitalist society, as Marx and Engels had predicted, but in an economically backward, quasi-feudal, predominantly agrarian society. The economic conditions were unfavourable for rapid socialist development. Corresponding to the country's economic backwardness was a cultural backwardness. The bulk of the Russian masses were illiterate, uneducated, superstitious and highly religious peasants. The working class, the vanguard of the revolution, comprised a minority. There were hardly any public educational establishments in the country. The tsarist government had destroyed many prior to the revolution. As such, Lenin observed that 'the political and social revolution preceded the cultural revolution, that very cultural revolution which nevertheless now confronts us' (1983: 100).

In 1919, Lenin mentioned 'how heavy the task of re-educating the masses was, the task of organisation and instruction, spreading knowledge, combatting the heritage of ignorance, primitiveness, barbarism and savagery that we took over' (1983: 50). The task of raising the masses' cultural level was immense. The regime basically needed to start the process from scratch. And it needed to do so immediately, since the cultural revolution was not only a precondition for raising the masses' political and class consciousness. It would also help them develop the productive forces and advance towards communism:

> We must raise culture to a much higher level. A man must make use of his ability to read and write; he must have something to read, he must have newspapers and propaganda pamphlets, which should be properly distributed and reach the people ... ceaselessly propagate the idea that political education calls for raising the level of culture at all costs.
>
> (Lenin 1983: 89–90)

Lenin showed an acute awareness of the ideological core of culture, as well as the problems this created for its development. Unlike political or military struggles, which could be won fairly swiftly with the right forces and organisation, the cultural struggle required a change in ideas, in class consciousness, and this could not be achieved through force of will. Such a change was, however, crucial for the political education of the working masses (Lenin 1983: 89–90).

By situating cultural development as the foundation for political education, Lenin highlighted the ideological and political function of culture in building socialism and communism. His basic point was that the workers needed to be able to read, write and comprehend basic ideological concepts if the state's written propaganda was to be effective in moulding communist citizens. An illiterate peasant would find little value in a pamphlet extolling the virtues of this or that party policy. They would become committed to the cause only if they could understand what was written for them. These works also needed to be widely available to the masses all over the country.

It was especially essential that the mass of backward peasants get organised into cooperative farming societies. These would constitute the basic units of socialist economic organisation in Soviet Russia. Once collectivisation was completed, the country would be 'standing with both feet on the soil of socialism'. In order for this organisation to be successful, however, it presupposed 'a standard of culture . . . precisely among the peasants as the overwhelming mass', one that, in turn, required 'a cultural revolution'. In essence, the peasants had to discard their petit-bourgeois attachments to individual farming allotments and embrace a more communal, collective organisation of farming and living. Only then would socialism be consolidated (Lenin 1983: 100).

Evidently, the cultural tasks facing Soviet Russia were immense. The country required a cultural revolution if it was to successfully build communism. Nevertheless, Lenin was confident that this revolution would succeed and for one reason: state power was in the hands of the working class for the first time in human history. This class was an inherently revolutionary and universal class. It could emancipate itself only if it developed the culture of both itself and the other labouring peoples:

> Nowhere are the masses of the people so interested in real culture as they are in our country; nowhere are the problems of this culture tackled so thoroughly and consistently as they are in our country; in no other country is state power in the hands of the working-class which, in its mass, is fully aware of the deficiencies, I shall not say of its culture, but of its literacy; nowhere is the working-class so ready to make, and

nowhere is it actually making, such sacrifices to improve its position in this respect as in our country.

(Lenin 1983: 99)

Since Russia lacked mass education establishments, Lenin viewed public libraries as the most effective means of educating the people as rapidly and as efficiently as possible. They could serve the most people in the shortest time. The development of a socialist public library service was an essential condition for the success of the socialist revolution and the transition to communism. It had to become the leading force, the vanguard, the teacher, in raising the masses' cultural level. If public libraries were not built, there would be no communism. Dobler made this clear in his article 'The Modern Library System', published in *Pravda* in 1921:

> At the present time the libraries are called upon to play a more important role than they did formerly. Formerly . . . libraries catered only for a very limited part of society owing to the enormous percentage of illiterates and all sorts of obstacles which were raised to the workers and peasants' striving for learning. Now the library must become one of the most important levers in public education, and for this reason the question of the system, i.e. the scheme according to which we shall have to locate and link together the institutions supplying the people with books, should interest everybody. To who books get in the first place, who makes most use of them, will depend on how the system is constructed.

(1983: 63)

'When in power', wrote Krupskaya, 'Vladimir Ilyich devoted much time to promoting the growth of the library network and equipping it as well as possible' (1968b: 9). With the help of the Communist Party and the working class, he guided the construction of the world's first socialist public library service for the people.

The leading role of the party

Lenin's most influential contribution to Marxism was the doctrine of *vanguardism*. He discovered, through his own experience in leading the Russian Revolutions, that the leading role of the Marxist Party was an *essential* condition for the success of the socialist revolution. For Lenin, therefore, the most important thing in building Soviet socialist public libraries was establishing the party's leading role over them. The party, by utilising Marxism, had to dictate, direct and set the course of library construction. The party had to be the vanguard, the guide and the architect of the entire process. Without this leadership, a public library service for the people would be impossible. At the same time, Lenin always emphasised that the vanguard party was a *working-class* party. It was composed of the brightest, most talented elements of the working class, and it was nothing without the support and confidence of this class. The workers had to check every step the party made and ensure that it fulfilled their demands. Lenin made this clear long before the October Revolution. In 1905, he argued that

> reading-rooms, libraries and similar establishments – must all be under Party control. The organised socialist proletariat must keep an eye on all this work, supervise it in its entirety, and, from beginning to end, without any exception, infuse into it the life-stream of the living proletarian cause.
>
> (1974: 46)

The October Revolution made this aim a reality. The party secured its hegemony over the cultural and educational sphere, including the public libraries. By doing so, it could ensure that these libraries began to serve the new ruling class in Russia – the proletariat (Lenin 1983: 52).

The party, as a general rule, exercised its influence not directly but indirectly. The revolution replaced the bourgeois parliamentary state with the Soviets, political organs of self-governance that the workers and peasants themselves established during the 1905 and 1917 Revolutions. The Soviet state was the main governing organ in Russia, and the party had to implement its directives through it. The Council of People's Commissars (Sovnarkom or SNK) was the highest executive body in the Soviet government, and the People's Commissariat for Education (PCE) led the library work. Since the Communist Party secured itself the position as the only legal party, however, its representatives assumed many of the leading Soviet positions. Lenin himself assumed the SNK's highest position as its chairman, whilst the Bolsheviks A. V. Lunacharsky and N. K. Krupskaya became the leader and deputy leader of the PCE, respectively.

The American–Swiss system

Lenin wanted Russia's public libraries to draw on the experience of the Western countries, where they were more developed. In November 1917, he remarked to Lunacharsky, '[W]e must take over from the advanced bourgeois countries all the forms of wide propagation of library books that have been evolved there'. It was necessary, he said, to 'call in library experts. A great deal of good is being done in that respect in America' (Lenin in

Lunacharsky 1983a: 176; and cited in Lunacharsky 1983b: 178). Lenin repeatedly endorsed what he called the 'Swiss-American system' (Lenin 1983: 40, 42, 131, 133, 137). This should be unsurprising, given that he had used Swiss libraries himself and because of his extensive research into the New York Public Library, which provided the basis for his 1913 article 'What Can Be Done for Public Education'. The essential features of the 'Swiss–American' system include quick service, free access to bookshelves, inter-library loan, general catalogues and branch libraries that can order books from the main library if needed (Dobler 1983: 63). In an article written shortly after the October Revolution titled 'The Tasks of the Public Library in Petrograd', Lenin pointed out that tsarism had left the city's library service 'in a very bad state'. As such,

> [t]he following changes, based on principles long practised in the free countries of the West, especially Switzerland and the United States, must be made immediately and unconditionally:
>
> (1) The public library (the former Imperial Library) must immediately start an exchange of books with all public and state libraries in Petrograd and the provinces and with foreign libraries (in Finland, Sweden, etc.).
> (2) The forwarding of books *from one library to another* must be made post-free by law.
> (3) The library's reading-room must be open, as is the practice with private libraries and reading-rooms for the *rich* in civilised countries, from 8.00 a.m. to 11.00 p.m. daily, not excluding Sundays and holidays.
>
> (Lenin 1983: 38)

Of course, Lenin did not want to simply ape the Swiss–American system. He and the other Bolsheviks were well aware that the public libraries in the capitalist countries pacified and excluded the working masses whilst catering to the middle and upper classes. Dobler, for instance, argued that the 'servile copying of the American model' would show a 'complete disregard for the practical needs of our reality' (1983: 63). Such an initiative would ignore the fact that America's 'open to all' public libraries were bourgeois. Indeed, the class-conscious workers in Russia realised this:

> As soon as the revolution broke out and the workers obtained greater opportunity to attend to their spiritual development, their own factory and works libraries started to grow like mushrooms, despite the fact

that no-one prevented the workers from going to the libraries open to all, that the doors were wide open . . . the workers did not conceive the desire to go there and make them their own.

(Dobler 1983: 64)

Rather than promote the wholesale adoption of the Swiss–American system, the party approached it dialectically. The old socialist aspects of capitalist public libraries had to be maintained whilst the reactionary bourgeois aspects had to be discarded. It was necessary to keep the aspects that served the working masses whilst discarding those that excluded them. As Krupskaya expressed it,

> [w]e must use the experience of the other countries, of capitalist countries, in every way we can; in technical reconstruction, in technical service to readers we must borrow all we can. But we must build our own library – a library of a different kind, more in keeping with our socialist way of life.
>
> (1968a: 46)

A socialist public library system

Regarding public libraries, Krupskaya emphasised that every effort had to be made to 'exhibit their specific socialist character', the 'socialist character of [their] work' (1968a: 50). Dobler (1983: 65) made the same point when he said that 'our library system, unlike the American, must consist not of libraries for all, but of . . . workers' libraries'. The essence of these statements was that the Soviet public libraries had to prioritise the working masses. The party and the state promoted several measures in order to realise this objective.

The first major policy concerned the national organisation of public libraries. When the Bolsheviks came to power, these were scattered, unconnected and independent. There was no standardisation in the service. There was 'no library system'. Public libraries had arisen 'not according to any plan' but according to the whims of various wealthy donors. This made them 'far below the requirements' of socialism (Dobler 1983: 63). In his article 'The Work of the People's Commissariat for Education', Lenin made a detailed analysis of this state of affairs. On one hand, he noted that 'the thirst for knowledge among the mass of workers and peasants' was 'tremendous'. In particular, 'the striving for education and the establishment of libraries' was 'mighty and 'popular' in the real sense of the word'. On the other hand, the state was 'still very short of ability in organising, regulating, shaping and properly satisfying this popular urge. Much remains to be done in creating a real *integrated network* of libraries' (Lenin 1983: 68). Lenin elsewhere added that 'this system must work according to a definite plan . . . and bring books closer to the worker and peasant reader' (1983: 57). This proposal found its definite expression during the First-All Russia Congress of Adult Education in 1919:

> At present we must combat the survivals of disorganisation, chaos, and ridiculous departmental wrangling. This must be our main task. We must take up the simple and urgent matter of mobilising the literate to combat illiteracy. We must utilise the books that are available and set to work to organise a network of libraries which will help the people to gain access to every available book; there must be no parallel organisations, but a single, uniform planned organisation. This small matter reflects one of the fundamental tasks of our revolution. If it fails to carry out this task, if it fails to set about creating a really systematic and uniform organisation in place of our Russian chaos and inefficiency, then this revolution will remain a bourgeois revolution because the major specific feature of the proletarian revolution which is marching towards communism is this organisation.
>
> (Lenin 1983: 52)

What did Lenin mean by a 'single, uniform, planned organisation'? The distinguished Soviet library scholar O. S. Chubaryan explains it as follows:

> The underlying concept of this system is that in every aspect of its activity each library is regarded as a component link in a state-wide chain of libraries. In practice, this means doing away with parochialism, second, the mutual exchange and use of one another's stocks of books which implies inter-library loan as an all-embracing state-maintained service, and third, the running of libraries in conformity with a state plan.
>
> (1972: 40)

In contrast to capitalist counties, where the public libraries functioned differently across the nation, depending on the arbitrary views of the management and local government councils, the Soviet system had to establish a centralised unitary system. In this system, the national centre –composed of the party and state – had to determine a long-term plan for each library, as well as the service as a whole. Establishing this system would be no easy feat. It had to be 'built anew, in conditions of acute book hunger and almost complete absence of trained library staffs' (Dobler 1983: 63). The regime was unperturbed, however, since it had the power to mobilise the masses' creative energies on a scale unprecedented in human history.

In June 1918, Lenin issued an SNK resolution *On Library Organisation*, which demanded that the PCE 'immediately . . . take the most drastic measures . . . to centralise library administration in Russia' (SNK 1968a: 37). In July, the SNK issued a decree *On Safeguarding Libraries and Book Depositories*, signed by Lenin. This demanded that all Russian libraries be supervised and registered by the PCE. It asserted, moreover, that 'the future of these libraries, their distribution, the placing of them at the disposal of the people, the stocking of them, and the establishment of new libraries', would be 'handled by a department for libraries' attached to the PCE. 'All institutions and organisations' listed as having 'libraries of any kind' were obliged to report the fact to the PCE library department immediately. The failure to do this would be 'considered a breach of revolutionary law and order' and would render 'the offender liable to prosecution' (SNK 1968b: 37–38).

An integral part of Russia's library centralisation was the nationalisation of the private libraries. Under tsarism, many of the largest libraries were privately owned by aristocrats and landowners, and the workers were excluded from them. After the October Revolution, Lenin stipulated that if private *special* library owners required them for professional use, they could keep them, provided that the PCE established 'an exact record and control' over such libraries. These owners were still obliged, however, 'to hand over all books presenting a great historical, scientific or literary interest to special public book depositories'. As for the private libraries that the former owners did 'not actually need', these were to be surrendered to the government, which would, in turn, give them to the public libraries. It was also necessary 'to requisition' for public access 'all libraries' belonging to those who had fled their homes to places occupied by the counter-revolutionaries or to places unknown (Lenin 1983: 53). The government was swift to implement this policy. In November 1918, the SNK delivered a decree, signed by Lenin, *On the Procedure for Requisitioning Libraries, Book Depositories and Books Generally*. Henceforth, the requisitioning process had to occur only with the PCE's knowledge. And when books were found in confiscated properties, they had to be given to the library section of the PCE or the local organs for national education, which would, in turn, report back to the PCE (SNK 1968c: 38).

In April 1920, the SNK issued a decree, again signed by Lenin, *On the Nationalisation of Stocks of Books and Other Printed Matter*. Book stocks and printed materials belonging to private individuals, cooperative and other institutions were 'declared state property (are nationalised)'. Individuals and organisations found 'guilty of concealing collections of books and other printed matter' would be prosecuted (SNK 1968d: 39).

Whilst Lenin had no intention of destroying academic, special and technical libraries, he did insist on opening them to the public and integrating them into the planned state system. In November, the SNK delivered a decree, signed by Lenin, *On the Centralisation of Libraries*. It announced that 'all libraries' were 'open to all' and were joined into 'a single library network throughout the RSFSR'. This network would establish a 'central interdepartmental library committee' composed of people from the PCE, the trade unions and the Political Directorate of the Revolutionary Military Council of the Republic. This committee had the power to establish libraries and change their status, work out and approve plans for redistributing book resources, extend the library network and set up special, technical and school libraries. All libraries in the unified library network would be stocked through local distribution committees, which received books from the central distribution committee attached to the state publishing house (SNK 1983: 148–149).

Krupskaya suggested the establishment of semi-special public libraries. These would serve as mid-level stepping-stones between the standard, general knowledge libraries, and the more specialised, technical libraries. They 'would encourage a technical outlook and give people a basic knowledge of the physics, chemistry and mathematics necessary for competence in a particular field of technology'. Once the masses gained that knowledge, they would find it easier to access the technical libraries (Krupskaya 1968a: 49).

In the party's view, the construction of socialism demanded that every book, every piece of printed material serve this purpose. The masses could not be exposed to publications espousing bourgeois ideas as this would corrupt their communist consciousness. In order to ensure that all the publicly available reading materials served socialism, the party demanded state control over every written publication in the country. In June 1920, the Sovnarkom issued a decree, signed by Lenin, *On the Transfer of Bibliographical Work in the RSFSR to the State Publishing House*. This gave the PCE responsibility for the registration of all printed matter published in Russia. Those who violated this resolution were 'liable to punishment on conviction in a people's court' (SNK 1968e: 40).

Krupskaya oversaw the books selected for the public libraries. Like Lenin, she argued that it was imperative to exclude 'harmful books from the people's libraries', 'libraries intended for the masses'. Shortly after the revolution, she noted that 'such literature still remained in the libraries at many places'. They retained 'much patriotic literature from the time of the war, and other propaganda material written on topics current in 1917, such as the Constituent Assembly and the like'. Moreover 'these libraries also contained many books and pamphlets interpreting decrees and laws which have long since been repealed; all of which was calculated to mislead the less-informed reader'. Krupskaya endorsed Pokrovsky's view that Soviet libraries sought 'the final establishment of positive atheism in the mind of man, and the spreading of propaganda for a comprehensive, logical, materialistic world-view'. However, she opposed the notion that every reactionary book deserved to be banned. For Krupskaya, the question of which reactionary books to permit depended on how popular they were. Those that the masses actually read required banning, whilst those that weren't being read could remain, since they could create no damage. Krupskaya established this rationale in an article published in *Pravda* in 1924. Here, she criticised the Commission for Book Revision for 'the fact that the list of excluded "religious" books was very limited'. The masses were attracted to religious books, and so it was important to exclude them. At the same time, she opposed the commission's decision to exclude the idealist philosophers – Plato, Kant, Ernst Mach and others – since the masses were not reading them. It was also a mistake to prohibit some of Tolstoy's and Kropotkin's works. To be sure, communists had no interest in popularising Tolstoy's religious worldview. His focus on individual self-improvement and non-resistance to evil was contrary to communism, an atheistic worldview that encouraged collective betterment and class struggles against oppression. And yet Tolstoy's sermons were 'powerless to convert anyone', since the average reader was 'already sufficiently saturated with collectivistic psychology' and 'imbued with the fighting spirit'. Kropotkin's anarchist ideas also posed no threat. The Soviet state had demonstrated the 'great power' of organisation and authority. The workers' own experience had 'made the teachings of Tolstoy and Kropotkin unreal and ineffectual', and so the prohibition of their works was unnecessary (Krupskaya 1924).

The public libraries also had to start holding more copies of the major educational texts. In the bourgeois libraries, it was permissible to provide only one or two textbooks for each subject, since a few educated middle-class individuals comprised the bulk of the readership. Under socialism, by contrast, the uneducated masses would be frequenting the libraries in droves, and so far, more textbooks were necessary in order to meet their demand for knowledge:

> By their composition the old libraries are adapted for the individual reader. They are not for the masses. Not without reason do we have the words duplicate, triplicate, etc., which librarians are in a hurry to get rid of. Just try to carry on a library today without quadruplicates and quintuplicates. We need 20–30 textbooks on every subject.
> (Pokrovsky 1983: 181)

Since there was a severe shortage of reading material in the country, compromises had to be made. In order to maximise what Dobler (1983: 64) called 'the extreme economy in the use of books', Lenin demanded that 'all books and newspapers be distributed gratis *only* to the libraries and reading-rooms, which provide a proper reading service for the whole country and the whole mass of workers, soldiers and peasants'. This, in his view, would 'accelerate, intensify and make more effective the people's eager quest for knowledge'. Education would 'advance by leaps and bounds'. It was essential, even in the country's 'state of poverty, to give the people two copies of a newspaper through each of the 50,000 libraries and reading-rooms, all the necessary textbooks and world classics, and books on modern science and engineering' (Lenin 1983: 70–72). Lenin tasked the Foreign Literature Committee with concentrating in each library 'one copy each of all the latest technical, scientific (chemistry, physics, electrical engineering, medicine, statistics, economics, etc.) magazines and books for 1914–1921 published abroad' (1983: 88). They also had to house documents and reports on 'production propaganda', 'matters of production', the 'single economic plan', 'the labour front' and 'the training of workers and peasants in administration'. These would 'serve to spread vocational training and *polytechnical* education' (Lenin 1983: 60–61, 76–77, 79). It was important that the masses acquire the habit of reading the regional economic conference reports, as published in the newspapers, magazines and pamphlets. 'Unless an increasing number of the population grow accustomed to reading these reports in the libraries, it is useless talking about transforming this semi-barbarous country into a cultured and socialistic one' (Lenin 1983: 96–97). Above all, it was essential for the public libraries to collect and house 'everything published by Marx and Engels' (Lenin 1983: 62). In the 1930s, during the reign of J. V. Stalin, Krupskaya suggested that

> [e]ither the works of Marx, Engels, Lenin and Stalin can be put on a separate shelf, without their works being linked with other topics; or else they can be put on special shelves but at the same time have individual articles by them put with the topics they illustrate; thus books on technology would be shelved alongside statements on technology by Marx, Engels, Lenin and Stalin. This ought to be done in the catalogues as well as on the shelves.
>
> (1968a: 51)

Given the dire circumstances in the fledging Soviet state, Lenin recognised that many of the targets for getting books into the libraries would not be achieved. Nevertheless, he reminded the defeatists of 'the simple truth that even a hundred copies' of a publication, 'distributed one to every Gubernia [an administrative sub-division in Russia] library and all the major state libraries, will provide a source of information for *the whole of Russia*' (Lenin 1983: 77).

In order to ensure an even more efficient use of books, and provide a greater convenience to the toilers, Lenin promoted travelling libraries. These would bring books to the masses where they lived and worked, thereby making things easier for those who had difficulty going to the libraries:

> The readers must be provided . . . with great mobility of books- the books must go to the reader of themselves. For this use will have to be made of the post and all kinds and forms of travelling libraries arranged. Most probably we are not going to have enough books for all the enormous mass of our people, among whom literacy will be growing and if we do not give books wings, do not increase their circulation over and over again, we shall have book starvation.
> (Lenin cited in Lunacharsky 1983b: 178)

When he advocated the extensive use of travelling libraries in 1918, 'Vladimir Ilyich set the task of arranging things so that any of the most learned books in the library could get into the hands of a working man anywhere'. As Pokrovsky, remembers, however, 'the task was too grand for the technical conditions of the time'. Transport and postal communications were disrupted, and 'the colossal system that Vladimir Ilyich was thinking of was then unfeasible'. To add to this, a few months after Lenin set this aim, the civil war arrived, and the government 'had to dispatch all over Russia not books, but Red Army Men, shells and machine guns'. Nevertheless, Pokrovsky describes Lenin's idea as 'one of the brightest that was suggested by the revolution'. Indeed, 'this old proletarian idea' was conceived in the 1870s by S. Khalturin. In an effort to bypass the repressive tsarist censors, he organised a system of illegal mobile libraries for the workers in St. Petersburg. Besides this, books were also sent to the workers who needed them in other parts of Russia:

> And that idea of a book, not as something dead, lying on a shelf, but something alive, which moves about over the whole country, which gets into the hands of the popular masses, that is what makes the sharp distinction between library organisation now and old.
> (Pokrovsky 1983: 180–181)

Dobler wrote extensively on the importance of travelling libraries. He emphasised that

> not a single valuable book must be idle like dead capital. Adaption of books and libraries to the needs of the workers is possible if we direct all our forces to work at the factories, works, tea-rooms, clubs and other

establishments where the working masses gather, taking the books to them and making readers and friends everywhere.

(Dobler 1983: 64)

The October Revolution gave the working class power over the largest country in the world. In general, the public libraries were bigger, better stocked and more plentiful in the urban areas than in the rural agricultural areas. This was one of the legacies of the division between town and country that the Soviet regime inherited from capitalism. As a result, the rural dwellers were generally at a far lower cultural level than those living in urban areas. Abolishing the distinction between town and country was a necessary condition for communism, and so the regime devoted enormous resources to this task. As Krupskaya explained, however,

> the gulf between the cultures of town and country, a relic of capitalism, is not removed by a wave of the hand. Its removal depends on the social structure, on prolonged and diligent work to raise the cultural standards of the country.
>
> (1968a: 46)

Lenin saw public libraries as the most effective means of overcoming this gulf, yet he recognised that it was infeasible to build permanent fully stocked library buildings in the rural areas immediately. The country lacked the resources. Lenin therefore attached special importance to the work of the travelling libraries and village reading huts. The latter, he said, would for a long time be the main source and almost the only institution for the political education of the rural masses. According to the Soviet librarian V. A. Modestov, Lenin spoke to him about the leading role of a competent, educated librarian, who must be provided with the necessary conditions for satisfying village requirements (1983: 191–192).

A new type of librarian

The transformation of Russia's scattered, unorganised, mostly private libraries into a centralised, integrated, planned public library system was only one aspect of the transition from bourgeois to socialist public libraries. The second change concerned the nature and role of the librarians themselves. These two aspects of the transition were interconnected. As Pokrovsky, explained, the change in the country's public library structure, in turn, demanded a change in their internal organisation, personnel and librarian–patron relations:

This change in the character of libraries, this transformation from dead depositories, kinds of archives of printed matter into a cultural, live mobile force which impregnates the masses, changes also the significance of the librarian. The librarian-custodian, the librarian-bookworm, who conserves these books, giving out this one or that one only at the request of those who need them – that librarian is doomed to die out, just as the whole of the old system is doomed.

(1983: 181)

The Soviet Union had to establish 'a new type of librarian', one who was not only 'a real educational worker' but also 'the prime educational worker'. Librarians had to be 'the necessary link connecting the masses with science and culture' (Pokrovsky 1983: 181).

This was another big task. Prior to the October Revolution, many of Russia's librarians were reactionaries who supported the Tsarist regime and capitalism. They typically treated the working masses with contempt and disgust. Lenin therefore argued that it was necessary 'to remove, *as a general rule* [emphasis in original], from the management of libraries the former owners of those libraries which have been placed at the disposal of the People's Commissariat for Education and made available for public use' (1983: 53). The old reactionary library staff needed replacing with new personnel from the Ministry of Education (Lenin 1983: 38). Since these personnel would have been vetted and approved by the Soviet state and party, their socialist credentials and proletarian outlook were guaranteed. Since a new army of communist librarians was required, Lenin charged the PCE 'with increasing the ... number of librarians of the public government state libraries' (1983: 53). There was no time for elaborate formal courses on librarianship, however. New staffs were needed immediately. As such, Dobler (1983: 65) proposed the creation of 'a permanent school for practitioners learning library organisation under the direction of an experienced library worker, not by means lectures but by the work itself'.

Krupskaya devoted significant attention to the characteristics, attitude, work ethic and role of socialist public librarians. She argued that they had to commit themselves to creating a 'real soviet system-to get to know their readers and to give them, not just a service, but the kind of service expected in a socialist society' (Krupskaya 1968a: 46):

We must bring our work nearer to the masses, and even change our way of speaking. To make free with special library terminology, as has been our custom, is not good enough. In our professional work we should avoid library jargon; we ought to speak so that not only the librarian understands, but also so that what is said is clear to the readers as well.

(Krupskaya 1968a: 47)

In the capitalist countries, 'library jargon' is the *sine qua non* of the traditional librarian and petit-bourgeois library scholar, who like to flout their professional status and pretend that their discipline is an elite science, beyond the comprehension of the masses. Krupskaya made it clear that there was no space for this kind of language and attitude under socialism. There was no room for pretentiousness amongst public librarians. They had to be the humble servants of the masses.

As Soviet society moved towards communism, Krupskaya urged librarians to 'make far higher demands of themselves' (1968a: 47). In particular, it was necessary to reject the bourgeois tendency to treat every reader as an abstract individual, independent of space and history. It was instead necessary to establish the class background and life circumstances of the patron. Only then could the librarian ascertain their needs:

> We must avoid considering the reader outside time and place, from an academic or general point of view, as is common in bourgeois library literature; he must be observed in the context of his working and domestic situation. The link between the readers needs and the age, the moment in time in which he lives, is a strong one, and one cannot generalise about a readers' demands except for a particular age, it is within the demands that arise from the socialist way of life within our country, and what is distinctive or special about them, that we are concerned.
> (Krupskaya 1968a: 47)

In order to ascertain what the readers needed, it was imperative to know the region they lived in and what forms of employment existed there. For instance, a worker employed in heavy industry living in an urban centre would have different tastes and needs from a peasant working on a collective farm in the countryside. The librarian had to identify these things in order to 'grasp' what the readers required (Krupskaya 1968a: 48).

Krupskaya insisted that librarians could not be politically unconscious. They could not pretend to be politically 'neutral'. They had to 'know basic Marxism-Leninism' as a *prerequisite* for working in the profession. Whenever the opportunity presented itself, librarians 'everywhere in the country' were obliged to 'passionately . . . offer to their readers the works of Marx and Engels' (Krupskaya 1968a: 48–49). Krupskaya also ridiculed the notion that book annotations 'ought not to include any kind of political evaluation' and 'that objectivity was all important'. These views were alien to Soviet Marxist librarianship. The approach to annotation

> must depend on the kind of annotation being made, and for what purpose. It may be that a simple annotation is sufficient merely for

arranging books, but that side by side with this annotation there ought to be a Marxist evaluation of the book. It is no simple matter to evaluate a book properly, but a large question and one must be a good Marxist to tackle it. Thus with every step do librarians feel how much they need to study Marxism-Leninism.

(Krupskaya 1968a: 48–49)

Krupskaya wanted librarians to constantly improve their work. This did not mean working longer hours. It meant working like the 'Stakhanovites', who were celebrated for their superior labour productivity, discipline and zeal. They had to emulate 'Stakhanov's business-like attitude to his work' and organisation. The socialist public library service had to 'be a model of efficiency', and in striving for this, it was necessary to draw 'draw on the experience of our colleagues' (Krupskaya 1968a: 51).

Regarding catalogues, librarians had to discard the approach of the narrow specialist. The readers needed catalogues, and not everyone was competent to use one. 'This mattered less in the days when readers were few and the librarian had time to attend to each one'. Under socialism, however, the workers would flood the libraries, and there was 'a special need to provide catalogues and handbooks and to ensure that readers know how to use them' (Krupskaya 1968a: 50).

In a letter to the PCE in 1919, Lenin proposed another method for ensuring that the public libraries acted like Stakhanovites and did their best to serve the masses. 'More than anything else', he said, 'the libraries, including of course reading huts, all kinds of reading rooms, etc., require *competition* between individual provincial libraries, groups, reading rooms, etc.'. In practice, this entailed the public libraries providing '1) authentic and complete *information* to the Soviet government and all citizens about what is going on; 2) enlisting the *public* in library work; 3) encouraging *competition* among library workers' (Lenin 1983: 46).

Measure (1) sought to make the public libraries more democratic. By providing information on their activities and organisation to the state, the party and the masses, the public libraries would remain transparent to everyone and accountable to the people. The party could ensure that they were performing their socialist tasks correctly and in accordance with the party line. Krupskaya explained how this accountability system worked in 1921. 'As a rule', she explained, 'libraries have library councils of representatives of the organized population: local Party cell, trade union, youth league, women's section, who see the correct functioning of libraries'. 'The village reading-rooms have 'councils of village reading-rooms' of local peasants' for the same function. The Central Library Committee of the country could publish circulars, obliging the councils to issue it certificates confirming that the right reading materials had been received and put to the correct use (Krupskaya cited in Lenin 1983: 92).

Measure (2) served another characteristic of socialist democracy – the constant 'active participation' of the working people in their public affairs, including the cultural and educational spheres. This entailed 'all-round help on the part of the Soviet power in the matter of the self-education and self-development of workers and working peasants' in the 'organization of libraries' (Lenin 1983: 48). The public libraries had to not only incorporate the masses' demands and suggestions but also involve them directly in the library's administration and management, on a daily and constant basis. This would encourage the masses to feel increasingly like the masters of their own cultural and educational institutions rather than its passive subjects. Lenin hoped that as the technological improvements simplified the library tasks over time, the untrained workers would be able to perform more of their functions, thereby eroding the distinction between librarians and patrons. Under communism, Lenin envisioned this distinction vanishing entirely. Librarianship as a 'profession' would wither.

Measure (3) sought to catalyse the growth of public libraries themselves and instil in them the correct socialist operational attitudes. Lenin encouraged the libraries to focus on improvements in the following areas:

> For example: 1) Can you supply precise information to prove more books have been lent from your library? or 2) how many people visit your reading room? 3) book and newspaper exchange with other libraries and reading rooms? or 4) compilation of a central catalogue? or 5) work on Sundays? or 6) work in the evenings? or 7) encouragement of new readers, women, children, non-Russians, etc.? or 8) satisfaction of readers' references? or 9) simple and practical means of storing books and newspapers? Saving them? Mechanical means of obtaining the book and returning it to its place? or 10) lending a book? Or 11) simplification of guarantees in lending a book? Or 12) sending it through the post?
>
> (1983: 46–47)

These metrics were concerned with either increasing the number of public library readers, increasing the business-like efficiency of the organisation or expanding its services. The libraries that made the most improvements and carried them out best of all would receive 'bonuses in the form of valuable books, collections, and so on' (Lenin 1983: 46). By providing these material incentives, Lenin hoped to create some comradely inter-library competition that would ensure their continuous, long-term development.

Socialist public libraries after Lenin

After Lenin's death in 1924, the party and state used his ideas as a theoretical basis for the continued construction of Soviet socialist public libraries. In December 1936, Krupskaya gave an introductory speech at the All-Union Conference on Theoretical Questions of Library Science and Bibliography. In her opening remarks, she said that 'in the library sector of our cultural front our work is made much easier by the detailed instructions of Vladimir Ilyich, who always showed great concern for library matters' (Krupskaya 1968a: 45). The CPSU made 'every effort . . . to consistently implement Lenin's plan'. In the late 1920s, the party's Central Committee declared that 'mass literature' had to 'play a more instrumental role than heretofore in mobilising the masses to tackle the main political and economic tasks'. This, in turn, 'required further advances in library management' (Chubaryan 1972: 25).

As the socialist economy and living standards rose, the public library network grew in tandem. By educating the masses in the various scientific and technological disciplines, they made an increasing contribution to industrialisation and collectivisation. The government invested heavily in the development and expansion of public libraries. By 1989, the Soviet Union had 360,000 libraries with 5.6 billion books, all featuring a modern organisation system. The state owned and ran 90 per cent of the libraries, whilst public organisations maintained the other 10 per cent. The number of readers reached 234 million (Petrosian 1989: 38; Chubaryan 1972: 26).

The state devoted significant resources to expanding the rural library network in order to eradicate the distinction between the town and countryside. Between 1925 and 1930, it initiated a 'library drive' focused on the rural areas with biggest book shortages. The masses responded enthusiastically. Factory workers, intellectuals and students 'donated hundreds of thousands' of their own books to establish more village public libraries. 'Each new library opened was an occasion of great rejoicing and festivity'. The drive was a resounding success. By 1972, 75 per cent of the country's public libraries were in the countryside, and there was one library for every 1500 rural citizens, as compared to one for every 2000 urban citizens. There were 537 books per 100 people. The readership was 180 million, compared to 3 million under tsarism. Over 90 per cent of factory workers, engineers, technicians, teachers and college and vocational students used the public libraries (Chubaryan 1972: 26–27).

Public library regulations in the USSR stated that every citizen could use the libraries without charge without any discrimination, and the libraries were obliged to furnish the readers with the books they wanted and satisfy the readers' requests (Chubaryan 1972: 27–28).

Under tsarism, the chauvinist Russian empire oppressed over a hundred nations and nationalities living within its borders by imposing on them ruthless 'Russification' cultural assimilation measures. The Soviet Union united these nations under one state, and the party endorsed a Marxist nationalities policy that oversaw the *harmonious development* of the different national cultures. The state provided libraries for the various nationalities, including books in their own languages. In contrast to tsarist times, when the libraries were centralised in Russia, the socialist state prioritised the construction of libraries in the national republics (Chubaryan 1972: 28–29).

For example, Tajikistan, before the revolution, had no libraries and no books or periodicals in the native language. By 1972, this republic had 3000 libraries. Before the revolution, there was nothing to read in the remote Chukotka Peninsula and no one who could read, since the natives had no written language. By 1972, every village had its own library, and the various national minorities had developed their own national literature. In the Sun Valley, public libraries were built containing publications on the region's native peoples' history, literature and production. These libraries sponsored cultural events that displayed books, samples of bone carving, embroidery and other local native handicrafts. They organised talks on the dialects of the region's natives and the history of local folklore. The libraries also held galas organised and directed by the natives themselves. Local native poets and storytellers played a leading role in these events (Chubaryan 1972: 29–30).

Prior to the revolution, the highland peoples of the northern Caucasus were illiterate and without a written language. The tsarist government did all it could to impede their cultural development. The authorities denied the residents' requests to build public libraries, and they instead promoted wine shops to keep them drunk and subdued. By 1972, there were 20 libraries in the region, which had produced more than 80 Soviet scientists, writers, artists and other notables (Chubaryan 1972: 30–31).

After Lenin's death, Soviet socialist libraries continued to promote economic, cultural, technological and scientific progress. 'The revolution spurred the public demand for libraries of a new type that would actively strive for humanitarian ideals, human rights, a more durable peace and justice'. By providing books and information for all, the public libraries ensured that reading for the purpose of self-education became one of the most effective forms of education (Chubaryan 1972: 32–33). Librarians themselves played an active role in this process, by helping the readers select books, navigate the shelves and get the most out of the books read. Many part-time volunteers helped out. Their help ensured that the libraries could provide readers with 'every conceivable kind of material needed for their diversified and increasingly more complex activities'. By continuously aiding the education of the people, the public libraries sought to develop each individual and keep them informed of the latest, scientific, technological and cultural developments (Chubaryan 1972: 34–35).

Soviet public libraries also aided the masses' political education. For instance, they promoted 'Lenin readings', 'a series of thematic displays, functions and talks on philosophical and political problems' that stimulated public interest in them. These initiatives resulted in more citizens reading the Marxist-Leninist classics. Many of the library cultural activities also had an 'internationalist character'. Besides examining local history, they organised displays, lectures and functions on foreign revolutionary figures, events and movements (Chubaryan 1972: 35–36).

As in Lenin's time, the Soviet socialist public libraries featured a system of 'centralised state management', headed by the Ministry of Culture. At the same time, it was 'characteristic of Soviet socialist democracy' that the libraries encouraged 'popular initiative . . . in every way'. Chubaryan explains that this was 'a genuine mass movement for their steady improvement and not just a spasmodic "do well" campaign'. Public library democracy contained two features. First, library users participated in the library's cultural enlightenment work and information service. Second, they helped in the collective running and supervision of the libraries in order to improve their services (Chubaryan 1972: 45).

Soviet libraries exchanged literature with 4000 libraries, publishing houses and scientific centres in 140 countries. Every year they sent 1.2 million books abroad whilst receiving 900,000 in turn. On average, every patron read 22 books a year. And the ratio was the same in the union republics, showing that the cultural levels of the country were similar across the country. Among the librarians, 70 per cent had either a higher or specialised secondary education (Petrosian 1989: 39).

The crowning jewel of the Soviet socialist public library service was the V. I. Lenin State Library, situated close to the Kremlin in Moscow. Originally the Rumyantsev Museum, it was renamed after the Bolshevik leader following his death. Between 1918 and 1921, thanks to the more than 1.5 million volumes received through the nationalisation of big private libraries, it more than doubled its holdings and acquired several valuable collections. By 1989, it had 36 million books, 2500 staff, a daily attendance of 10,000, and an average of 40,000 books lent per day. This made it 'one of the biggest in the world' (Petrosian 1989: 1989). It contained a complex of reading rooms with special stocks in each, rooms for researchers in the various disciplines and special facilities for musicologists, students of rare material, art lovers and more. The section on rare materials contained numerous first editions of the writings of Marx, Engels and Lenin and other classics (Chubaryan 1972: 68–71). From the early days of Soviet rule, the

Lenin library 'led every effort and initiative to improve Soviet library services'. It acted as

> the centre of methodological guidance in such matters as long-range development planning, co-ordination of methods, the effort to raise the ideological and theoretical level of the popularisation and guidance in reading and making known the noteworthiest achievements in library management.
>
> (Chubaryan 1972: 72)

Soviet socialist libraries were not flawless. During the early days of the revolution, some librarian personnel retained the bourgeois attitudes of their capitalist counterparts. Krupskaya recalled a story told to her about a comrade who went to a technical library, which the Soviet government had made public. The librarian there was contemptuous that a workingman should visit a library intended for technical staff and spoke to him in Latin. When, in another public library, he asked for help finding some material, the librarian told him, '[S]eek and ye shall find!' (Krupskaya 1968a: 49–50). These bourgeois mentalities need to be rooted out, and they *were* gradually rooted out in proportion as the socialist system developed. No Soviet librarian was under the utopian illusion that the public libraries could be perfected under socialism, in a society riven by class differences. It was generally acknowledged that public library would serve the whole people consistently and comprehensively only under communism, the future classless society. As it turned out, the Soviet Union never attained this objective. Following the country's collapse in 1991, the public library system reverted back to capitalism.

But socialist public libraries are not dead. They live on today in China, Cuba, Vietnam, Laos and North Korea. In these countries, the ruling Workers' Parties are carrying forward Lenin's Marxist principles of public library management. First, and most important, they have shown complete fidelity to the working class in all their activities. When making any decision, their primary concern is whether it will meet the interests and needs of the working class. Second, they have remained loyal to Marxism-Leninism as the only guide to library construction. They have striven to construct a centralised, planned library system under the leadership of a revolutionary Marxist vanguard. These fundamental principles, which guide every Marxist-Leninist library, also underly the Vanguard library outlined in Chapter 5.

The Marxist-Leninist countries are not carrying forward Lenin's principles dogmatically, however. They are not uncritically copying the Soviet road. Lenin himself always emphasised that Marxism is not a dogma but a guide to action (Pateman 2019a). Marxism demands that socialist strategies, tactics and policies be applied creatively in accordance with the concrete conditions. Bearing this fact in mind, the socialist countries have creatively developed their own public library services in different ways. Of all of them, North Korea's is perhaps the most distinct yet also the least known. That is why the next chapter focuses on this secretive system.

References

Chubaryan, O. S. (1972) *Libraries in the Soviet Union*. Moscow: Novosti Press Agency Publishing House.

Dobler, F. (1983) 'The Modern Library System', in V. I. Lenin (ed.) *Lenin and Library Organisation*, pp. 62–65. Moscow: Progress Publishers.

Dudley, E. (1968) 'Introduction', in S. Simsova (ed.) *Lenin, Krupskaya, and Libraries*, pp. 7–8. London: Clive Bingley.

Krupskaya, N. K. (1924) 'A Bolshevist Index Expurgatorious', *Marxist Internet Archive* [online]. www.marxists.org/history/ussr/government/pravda/1924/04/09.htm

────── (1968a) 'We Shall Fulfil Lenin's Instructions on Library Work', in S. Simsova (ed.) *Lenin, Krupskaya, and Libraries*, pp. 45–51. London: Clive Bingley.

────── (1968b) 'What Lenin Wrote and Said about Libraries', in S. Simsova (ed.) *Lenin, Krupskaya, and Libraries*, pp. 9–10. London: Clive Bingley.

Lenin, V. I. (1974) *Collected Works*, Vol. 10. Moscow: Progress Publishers.

────── (1983) *Lenin and Library Organisation*. Moscow: Progress Publishers.

Lunacharsky, A. V. (1983a) 'Books to All Parts of Russia', in V. I. Lenin (ed.) *Lenin and Library Organisation*, p. 176. Moscow: Progress Publishers.

────── (1983b) 'Reminisces of the October Revolution', in V. I. Lenin (ed.) *Lenin and Library Organisation*, pp. 177–178. Moscow: Progress Publishers.

Modestov, V. A. (1983) 'Memorable Conversations', in V. I. Lenin (ed.) *Lenin and Library Organisation*, pp. 190–193. Moscow: Progress Publishers.

Pateman, J. (2019a) 'Lenin without Dogmatism', *Studies in Eastern European Thought*, 71: 99–117.

────── (2019b) 'V. I. Lenin on Library Organisation in Socialist Society', *Library and Information History*, 35/2: 98–109.

Petrosian, G. (1989) *Cultural Life*. Moscow: Novosti Press Agency Publishing House.

Pokrovsky, M. N. (1983) 'Opening Speech at the First Library Congress of the R.S.F.S.R', in V. I. Lenin (ed.) *Lenin and Library Organisation*, pp. 179–181. Moscow: Progress Publishers.

SNK (1968a) 'On Library Organisation', in S. Simsova (ed.) *Lenin, Krupskaya, and Libraries*, p. 37. London: Clive Bingley.

────── (1968b) 'On Safeguarding Libraries and Book Depositories', in S. Simsova (ed.) *Lenin, Krupskaya, and Libraries*, pp. 37–38. London: Clive Bingley.

────── (1968c) 'On the Procedure for Requisitioning Libraries, Book Depositories and Books Generally', in S. Simsova (ed.) *Lenin, Krupskaya, and Libraries*, p. 38. London: Clive Bingley.

—— (1968d) 'On the Nationalisation of Stocks of Books and Other Printed Matter', in S. Simsova (ed.) *Lenin, Krupskaya, and Libraries*, p. 39. London: Clive Bingley.

—— (1968e) 'On the Transfer of Bibliographical Work in the RSFSR to the State Publishing House', in S. Simsova (ed.) *Lenin, Krupskaya, and Libraries*, p. 40. London: Clive Bingley.

—— (1983) 'On the Centralisation of Library Organisation in the R.S.F.S.R', in V. I. Lenin (ed.) *Lenin and Library Organisation*, pp. 148–149. Moscow: Progress Publishers.

4 Kim Il-Sung and socialist public libraries in North Korea

Introduction

Although the Marxist socialist states have each developed different public library systems, North Korea's is the most distinct amongst them. The reasons for this are ideological. Whereas China, Cuba, China, Vietnam and Laos retained Marxism-Leninism, the Democratic People's Republic of Korea (DPRK) developed a new ruling ideology called *Juche*, meaning 'subject' or 'self-reliance'.

The relationship between Juche and Marxism-Leninism has been widely misunderstood. On one hand, Western commentators tend to argue that North Korea abandoned Marxism-Leninism long ago and that its governing ideology now resembles a form of Confucianism, ethnonationalism or quasi-religion. On the other hand, North Korean social scientists initially presented Juche merely as the creative application of Marxism-Leninism to the country's national conditions. Both views are incorrect. Juche is not simply a variant of Marxism-Leninism. It is a new ideology that formulated original principles. Nor is Juche unrelated to Marxism-Leninism. Juche has Marxism-Leninism at its *premise*. Juche upholds and maintains the revolutionary working-class essence running through Marxism-Leninism. Both doctrines have set themselves the task of building a socialist and communist society by utilising the ideas of Marx, Engels and Lenin. That is why North Korea – a socialist country based on Marxism – is well placed in a book on public libraries and Marxism. An examination of this system can illustrate the wide variation amongst public library services in socialist countries. It can also provide some unique insights into how to build a library service for the working class.

On the basis of Juche, its unique Marxist-inspired ideology, North Korea has developed an equally unique socialist public library service, one whose peculiar characteristics warrant a dedicated examination. That being said, little is known about North Korea's public libraries. This is because the DPRK is one of the most isolated and secretive countries on earth. Few people are allowed in or out. Observers have described this socialist state pejoratively as the 'hermit kingdom', since the ruling Workers' Party of Korea (WPK) deliberately prevents any significant contact with the outside world. Its nuclear arsenal and widely criticised 'totalitarian' practices have further contributed to its pariah status and separation from the capitalist world.

Acquiring information on North Korea's public libraries is difficult. Foreigners cannot simply cross the border and wander into any library they like. In fact, visitors cannot even explore the country as they like. Most visits take the form of tightly controlled tours. State-appointed guides cart people from destination to destination and then take them back to the official foreigners' hotel in the evening, which they cannot leave until the next day's tour. Even the slightest deviation from the carefully chosen itinerary is usually prohibited. It should therefore be unsurprising that scholarly discussions of the DPRK's librarians, libraries and library system are in short supply, rather generalised and full of unverified assumptions.

The main analysis is still Marc Kosciejew's (2009a, 2009b) two-part study, published in 2009. Kosciejew based this study on two sources: his strictly monitored and brief visitors' tour of North Korea's national library – the Grand People's Study House – in addition to the scant information released by the North Korean government. Kosciejew (2009a: 167) complained that his tour 'was oppressively monitored . . . tightly controlled, planned and supervised' and that since the book stacks were 'closed to everyone', he could 'not examine any of the collections'. Nevertheless, he felt confident enough to claim that his study established a 'foundation on which to build knowledge of North Korean libraries'.

This claim is unwarranted. Kosciejew's unscientific, subjective, biased assumptions become clear from the title of his study: 'Inside an Axis of Evil Library'. This title uncritically buys into the Western bourgeois moral evaluation of North Korea as a 'rogue state', which, in turn, ignores the crimes and atrocities of Western imperialism. The article's content regurgitates the same ideological tropes. Kosciejew's first words are that 'the traditional goal of western libraries is a commitment to advancing democracy through an informed citizenry'. By contrast, 'North Korean libraries . . . are not democratic institutions and do not subscribe to or reach for any democratic goals' (Kosciejew 2009a: 167). On one hand, therefore, Kosciejew erroneously presents bourgeois democracy and the bourgeois public library as pure, above-class phenomena, and on the other hand, he crudely juxtaposes this to the supposedly undemocratic North Korean system, which also lacks class characteristics. Kosciejew overlooks the fact that Western democracy and its public libraries serve capitalism. He neglects the fact that North Korea subscribes to its own socialist conception of democracy. Kosciejew's otherwise valuable insights are undermined by his Western ideological prejudices and his tendency to ignore the social substance underlying the phenomena of democracy and the public library.

Given the high prevalence of these kinds of biased evaluations of the DPRK, it is especially essential to examine its public libraries *from the perspective of North Koreans themselves*. Only this approach can safeguard the analysis from imperialist conceptions and moral values. Only this approach facilitates a deeper understanding of the library system established in one of the most misunderstood nations on earth. This chapter aims to provide such insight by examining the pronouncements of Kim Il-Sung, the leader of the WPK and the founder of the country. Long before his death, North Koreans began viewing Kim Il-Sung not only as the father of the nation but as the human embodiment of it. The man now known as the 'Eternal President' *became* North Korea, and as the leader of the WPK, he was both the de jure and de facto supreme ruler of the country. Kim Il-Sung's words and proclamations became the law. For this reason, his pronouncements provide an insight not only into his own view of public libraries but also the contemporary North Korean public library system. Indeed, in his reminisces, speeches and articles, the Eternal President showed a passion for public libraries that few other national leaders have matched. His son and successor Kim Jong-Il also devoted significant attention to the nation's public library system, and as such, his contribution is explored too.

This chapter begins by examining Kim Il-Sung's teenage years, when he used libraries to advance his early ideological education and political radicalism. It then looks at Kim's programme for public library organisation during the construction of socialism in North Korea. Kim emphasised the role of libraries in raising the knowledge level of the populace and also imbuing society with a *monolithic* communist ideology. The third section focuses on the Grand People's Study House and Kim's role in conceiving it. He saw this building as the embodiment of North Korea's cultural achievements and self-reliance. The fourth section compares and contrasts the DPRK's public library system to those of the Marxist-Leninist states. Such a comparison can showcase the rich diversity of public library systems in the world of Marxism-Leninism. Finally, the conclusion draws on the DPRK's public library philosophy in order to outline a guiding principle of the Vanguard library, which is outlined in Chapter 5.

The young Kim Il-Sung and libraries

Kim Il-Sung was born in 1912 to a poor Korean family in a small village near Pyongyang, the nation's capital. Like many Korean families, they resented the Japanese imperialist occupation of the peninsula, which began in 1910. Japanese colonial oppression forced the Kim family to migrate to the Republic of China in 1920, which was then a capitalist country. It was here, whilst living in the Manchurian province of Jilin, that the young Kim discovered his passion for libraries. It was here that he discovered their revolutionary potential.

From around age of 14, Kim paid a monthly fee to attend his local library, despite the fact that he was poor and lacked the money even for shoes. He claimed to stop there on his way home from school every day to spend hours reading books and newspapers. This enabled him to read various publications at little cost. When Kim could not afford to buy the 'good' books on sale in bookshops, he persuaded rich students to buy them 'and would borrow them from the sons of families who bought books not for reading but for the sake of displaying them in bookcases' (1994a: 206).[1]

From a young age, Kim noticed the class nature of libraries under capitalist systems. He consciously distinguished between the *buying* of books, which was a typically middle-class privilege, and the *borrowing* of books, which was the only viable option for poor people like him. The middle classes bought new books in the bookshops, whilst the workers and peasants went to the library to read used books if they could afford it, or they borrowed their books from the wealthy. Kim realised that book borrowing, a key function of libraries, enabled the lower classes to read and educate themselves.

In 1927, Kim Il-Sung joined the second-year class of the Jilin Yuwen middle school. Being a private school established by the newly emerging public circles in the country, it was comparatively progressive. During his time there, Kim rejected the feudal traditions of older-generation Koreans and became increasingly interested in communist ideologies, Marxism-Leninism in particular. He was 'more keen on reading the works of Marx, Engels, Lenin and Stalin than studying the school subjects'. Kim notes that the administration of school affairs was democratic. This extended even to the library, where a general meeting of students elected a chief librarian every six months. The chief was supposed to draw up a management plan for the library and also acquire books. Kim was elected chief librarian twice, and he used the opportunity to amass a 'large stock of Marxist-Leninist books'. He complained that with so many books available, he lacked the time to read them all (1994a: 206–207). Nevertheless, he managed to read several of the classics, including the *Communist Manifesto*, *Capital*, the *State and Revolution* and *Wage Labour and Capital* (FLPH 2001: 10). By making 'Marxist-Leninist literature and progressive books on socio-political matters' available to all in the library, Kim argues that he and many of his fellow students 'became firmly resolved to destroy landlords and capitalists and overthrow the unfair social system'. In utilising the school library for this purpose, 'our willpower became strong, and our revolutionary reserve grew firm' (1986a: 184). For Kim, then, the library was of crucial importance in facilitating his formation as a communist. He used it as an instrument of radical political education. The library enabled him and other poor students – who could not otherwise afford books – to read the socialist classics and develop themselves in a revolutionary direction.

In middle school, Kim Il-Sung established the Anti-imperialist Youth League with a group of like-minded students and organised a secret reading circle. Its mission and aim were to arm progressive young people with Marxist-Leninist theory and to then apply this theory in the struggle for Korean independence. This organisation grew quickly and expanded to many schools in the city. With the increase in the number of members, the group acquired a room at a local rice mill run by supporters of the Korean independence movement. One of the first things they did was open a library there. Kim wanted the library to be a centre of Marxist ideological education and a breeding ground for Korean communists (1994a: 210–211).

Kim recalls that it was no easy task building a library from scratch in those days. Most of the students were poor and had nothing but their bare hands. They managed to install bookshelves using boards they obtained from various places. But they still needed to supply the library with a stock of books and install desks and chairs (1985a: 48–49). In order to raise the money for these items, they worked on the weekends. The boys carried sleepers on their shoulders at the railway construction site or gravel on their backs at the riverside, whilst the girls cleaned rice at the rice mills. By doing this, the group earned enough to visit a large bookshop several times a week and buy 'armloads of books for the library'. In addition to stocking the standard range of books, they also installed a secret bookshelf to keep 'revolutionary books'. Once they finished equipping the library, they put up notices with brief book reviews throughout the city in the hope of enticing students. Kim Il-Sung wrote that their efforts were successful: 'a great many students hastened to call at our library' (1994a: 212, 214).

The library began by providing lots of love stories to attract students and interest them in reading. 'Needless to say', wrote Kim, 'these stories expressed reformist ideas but, on the other hand, they also contained some things which helped to stir up dissatisfaction with society. Therefore, although they were love stories, they were not so bad'. After students got interested in reading, Kim and the other politically conscious members gave them books on the social sciences. Then, when they had become ideologically awakened and educated through reading these books, they were given the 'revolutionary' books that were kept on the hidden bookshelves. These were usually books published in China or the Soviet Union (1985a: 48–49). They consisted mainly of the Marxist-Leninist classics, revolutionary stories and novels (1994a: 212). After borrowing these books, students had to comply with certain conditions before retuning them: they were obliged to return the books with written notes on the contents and their impressions of them (1985a: 48–49). This policy ensured that the students actually read and assimilated the contents of the books they borrowed.

Besides providing students with books, the library also hosted educational courses and lectures on various political subjects concerning Marxism and the Korean independence movement (1994a: 228). Since Kim Il-Sung played a leading role in the establishment, maintenance and organisation of the library, his friends called him 'Librarian Kim' or simply 'the Librarian' (1994b: 418).

But Kim was not content with merely educating people in Marxism. 'Having formed and built up our organizations we launched our practical struggle' against Japanese imperialism in Manchuria and Korea (1994a: 272). Once the library organisation had amassed sufficient members, he used it as a base of operations in planning this struggle, which began with a school strike protesting against Japanese rule in Korea. In response to these activities, the 'reactionary teachers' in the school responded harshly. They labelled Kim's activities as communist propaganda, thereby creating the pretext for repression. They raided the school library and seized the 'progressive' books there (1994a: 275).

In spite of this, Kim continued using the underground library at the rice-cleaning mill to educate poor students in Marxist-Leninist theory. His formal education ended in 1930 when he was arrested for subversive activities. Kim went on to join the Communist Party of China, and his activities shifted to more of a focus on guerrilla actions. Nevertheless, Kim would not forget the political and ideological function of libraries. During his teenage, years he gained first-hand experience in developing this function, and it determined his approach to public library organisation in the years to come.

Kim Il-Sung on public library organisation in North Korea

After Japan surrendered in 1945, Korea was divided into a Soviet-ruled north and an American-ruled south. By this point, Kim Il-Sung had proved himself a capable communist revolutionary, and the Soviets therefore installed him as the leader of the North Korean communists. After several years of negotiation and struggle, the Democratic People's Republic of North Korea was proclaimed in 1948, with Kim as the Soviet-designated premier. As the chairman of the ruling WPK, the Great Leader obtained effective control over the fledgling one-party socialist state.

One might assume that Kim Il-Sung would not be interested in public libraries from 1948 onwards. After all, national leaders have not typically shown much interest in library matters. This assumption would be mistaken. Kim devoted a great deal of attention to public library organisation in this period. He saw them as a key facilitator of socialist construction. In order to understand his approach to socialist public library organisation, however, it is, first, helpful to outline his guiding political philosophy.

From the beginning of his premiership, Kim Il-Sung argued that the Korean state could not dogmatically copy the interpretation of Marxism-Leninism developed and applied to the Soviet Union. If the nation was to successfully grow into a prosperous socialist society, then it had to establish its own guiding ideology, one that suited the specific conditions prevailing in the country whilst simultaneously inheriting the revolutionary ideas of Marxism-Leninism. Kim therefore developed Juche. The foundational principles of this philosophy are national self-reliance, independence and autonomy within the framework of a socialist state. In making these principles the centre of his political philosophy, Kim adhered firmly to J. V. Stalin's theory that it was possible to build socialism in one country. Juche maintained that the nation, and everyone within it, should strive for self-reliance whilst furthering the common good.

Kim wanted his unique ideology to permeate every aspect of Korean society. It was imperative, in his view, that the country could stand on its own two feet and without assistance from the outside. A fundamental condition for national self-reliance was a highly educated and knowledgeable population. Knowledge of science, technology and engineering were of particular importance. If the Korean people knew the latest discoveries in these fields, then they would be able to develop the productive forces of society by themselves and thereby meet the material needs of the nation (1995: 108–109).

Kim viewed knowledge to be so important that he insisted on its symbolic representation at the centre of the WPK's logo. Between the hammer, which represents the working-class, and the sickle, which represents the peasantry, the brush represents the intelligentsia, who would aid the workers and peasants with their cutting-edge knowledge. Kim Il-Sung viewed librarians as a part of this intelligentsia. By providing books and information to the masses, they could raise the educational and cultural achievements of the country.

The problem in Korea was that the masses were neither educated nor knowledgeable in the areas that interested Kim. Like Russia after the October Revolution, the country was a predominantly agrarian peasant nation with a low level of industrial development. Few people had even a basic level of formal education. The majority were illiterate, uninformed and steeped in religious superstition. Peasants worked in the fields with oxen and plough, barely producing enough food to feed themselves and their families. North Korea was, for all intents and purposes, *medieval*.

If the masses remained uneducated, illiterate and uninformed, then it would be impossible to develop the productive forces of society and build communism. Kim Il-Sung therefore called on all the working people to make it their daily routine and habit to study and raise their technical and cultural levels. He sought to establish 'a revolutionary habit of study throughout the country under the slogan of "the party, the people and the army all must study!"' (1991: 95).

The raising of scientific and technical knowledge was only one side of the Juche coin. Kim also wanted to imbue the entire North Korean population with his interpretation of communist ideology. If the country was to be both independent *and* united, then everyone had to assimilate the Juche political philosophy (1993: 355). Kim therefore viewed North Korean education as an inherently ideological and political affair. The whole of society had to understand and support the political ideals of himself and the party.

The young North Korean state possessed few educational or information establishments. The country was economically underdeveloped and poor. The government could not afford to purchase books for everyone. Because of this, Kim Il-Sung argued that public libraries had to be the leading force in educating the masses. They were the most effective means of giving knowledge to the masses as quickly and as cheaply as possible. By bringing scientific and ideological education to the masses, the libraries would serve an important political function. They would help build and consolidate the communist system.

Even before the formal establishment of North Korea, Kim Il-Sung called for a nationwide programme of public library construction across the country (1980a: 116). In 1947, in his concluding speech at a meeting of the Central Committee of the WPK, Kim delivered a talk, *On Developing Art and Literature and Activating Mass Cultural Work*. In this talk, Kim set forward the policy of establishing state control over all the 'libraries of the Japanese imperialists', as well as the building of 'new facilities of mass culture in the service of the masses of the people' (1980b: 381). The party immediately followed his behest, and the results were dramatic. According to Kim, Korea had only seven libraries under Japanese rule, and these were little more than book rooms. But by the end of 1946, there were 35 libraries and 717 reading rooms. And in 1948, the country had 103 libraries (1980b: 93, 1981a: 242). These figures are staggering for a country that had so few economic resources. They were made possible by the WPK, which used its centralised political control over the country to harness and mobilise the masses in the service of its long-term plans.

In his report to the Second Congress of the WPK, Kim requested the establishment of publicly accessible *party libraries* by the provincial, city and county party committees, in addition to the placing of party documents in all the public libraries. These would explain and bring home the party's policies to both its members and the masses and 'equip them with Marxist-Leninist ideology' (1981a: 216). Kim also called for the libraries to hold regular political and current affairs lectures, scientific seminars and public discussions and to start various group activities on a wide scale (1988: 378). These measures clearly show that he valued the *political* function of socialist libraries.

In 1953, after the Korean War ravaged the country, Kim Il-Sung argued that it was necessary to 'improve library work' and called for the state library in the capital to be restored and expanded. He demanded that the national economic plan should provide for the building of libraries in the provincial and town areas (1981b: 34). Kim wrote that there was no need to build big, local libraries in these areas. 'Simply taking a few rooms of a house and installing books in them' would serve this purpose (1988: 409).

In order to help teachers and students study, Kim called for the importation of over 1 million foreign books and the organisation of the central library in Pyongyang immediately after the Korean War armistice, 'while the country was reduced to ashes and people were still living in huts'. He recalls that

> [w]hen we told people of a foreign country that we wanted to buy these books, they were surprised. They exclaimed that, in spite of the acute shortage of food and clothing, the Koreans were buying books to train their own cadres rather than requesting food and clothing.
> (1986a: 521–522)

A problem with importing foreign books was that most Koreans could not read a foreign language. Kim sought to deal with this issue by calling on the mass translation of these books. In particular, he tasked every teacher, university lecturer and intellectual in the country to translate one book each. Kim Il-Sung argued that there was no need to translate books on social science, since most of these were reactionary and opposed to socialism. It was instead important to translate books on natural science in order to help the development of science and technology in the country (1989: 113).

Kim called for the maintenance of the public reading rooms. The reading tables required desk lamps and the floors required carpets (1982: 317). He also wrote that every cooperative farm should install a reading room for studying 'revolutionary history'. He requested that the farms rearrange their rooms so that farmers could acquire scientific and technical expertise on the job (1987: 27).

Kim Il-Sung saw no contradiction in communist education in bringing out reactionary books from the past and giving them to the people via the public libraries. 'The people's reading of these books will not weaken communist education', he wrote. 'The people who are armed thoroughly with out party's Juche idea and have acquired a firm revolutionary outlook on the world can analyse things of the past correctly from a critical working-class point of view' (1986b: 24). Nevertheless, Kim Il-Sung recognised that public libraries played an important role in shaping people's ideas. He criticised the 'wicked men who had infiltrated the party' who encouraged the people to read works that represented 'the interests of landlords and capitalists' and which spread 'capitalist and feudal-Confucian ideas'. Regarding foreign books, he called attention to 'some undesirable elements' who imported 'various reactionary books in order to spread revisionism and bourgeois ideas among our people' (1986b: 24–25, 28). Kim was furious when he found out that a provincial public library was 'still stocking a number of feudalistic books and bad books written by anti-party factionalists'. This showed that 'the revolutionary wind' had not swept through that public library (1986a: 525–526). At his behest, the party gave instructions that reactionary publications were not to be imported (1986b: 28).

For similar reasons, Kim was suspicious of requests to let foreign countries build libraries in North Korea. He claimed that the US and other imperialist countries were installing scientific libraries in the socialist countries in order to carry out their 'ideological and cultural infiltration' there. They did this 'under the cloak of 'exchange' and 'cooperation', saying that there were no national boundaries in science and technology (1985b: 334). In the cultural field, Kim was far more suspicious of cooperation with the capitalist countries than other communist leaders.

Kim Il-Sung did not want the libraries to house books that could imbue the masses with anti-communist, anti-Juche ideology. In 1970, in a discussion, *On Some Questions about Dealing with our National Cultural Heritage*, he wrote that 'we must examine all the books on our history and the classical works of our literature and art as soon as possible, and distinguish between those that are detrimental, and those which are beneficial, to the revolution'. Those that were beneficial to communism were to be made publicly available, whilst those that were detrimental were suitable only for 'limited readers' and were to be 'kept in special libraries for their use'. In order to carry out this work, Kim called for a 'State Evaluation Commission' consisting of senior party officials, government bodies and educational, scientific, literary and art institutions. He tasked this commission with examining the classical works of literature, art and the books of the history of the country and then adopting necessary measures (1986b: 27). Like all the other public institutions in society, the public libraries had to develop only those ideas that advanced the socialist consciousness of the masses.

During his 45 years in office, Kim Il-Sung moulded the emergent North Korean public library system in accordance with his Juche philosophy. He made it the task of the WPK, as the vanguard of the nation, to determine every aspect of library organisation, from their hiring practices to their in-house services and collections development. Every book, every workshop and every library employee was chosen by the party, and library workers had to be party members as a condition for practising their profession. In this way, the system of control from the party leadership down to the smallest library was complete and unimpaired. This centralised top-down system remains in force to this day.

What is more, Kim Il-Sung ensured that libraries served not only as institutions of general knowledge, technical and scientific education but also as institutions of ideological and political indoctrination. They were established with the explicit intention of imbuing the people with the WPK's Juche ideology. Every citizen was obligated to frequent their local library and study the party's documents and the Juche idea. Libraries were and remain as *political* institutions. They contribute to the maintenance of what Kim himself called a 'monolithic ideological system' (1985c: 119).

The Grand People's Study House

Today, the most spectacular icon of North Korean librarianship is the Grand People's Study House (GPSH), which serves as the national library of the country. Kim Il-Sung played a leading role in the development of this library, which was built in honour of his seventieth birthday in 1982. As Kim put it in 1988, 'I once said that if we raised enough money, we should build a Grand Peoples Study House, so that not only university graduates, but also everyone else could study there' (1996: 127). He made the construction of the building a central part of the nation's Second Seven-Year plan, which his son Kim Jong Il supervised (1988: 544). 'Under the guidance of the Party a magnificent building was rapidly constructed for the Study House' (1991: 379–380).

Some officials wanted to call the GPSH the Kim Il-Sung Study House. The Great Leader disagreed. 'In Korea', he argued, everything was 'geared towards the promotion of the people's wellbeing'. Everything in the country served the people, and so it was necessary to name establishments after the word 'people', 'like . . . the Grand People's Study House' (1999: 373). Kim Jong-Il claims that this decision showed 'a fundamental difference between the people-centred socialism of our own style and capitalism'. It showed brilliantly the 'people-oriented policy' of Kim Il-Sung and the party (Kim Jong-Il 2014: 238).

Kim also decided the location of the GPSH:

> A long time ago, when I approved the master plan for the construction of Pyongyang, I gave instructions that a spot was set aside for the construction of the Grand People's Study House, and I ensured that the Study House was actually built at that site.
>
> (1991: 379–380)

This spot is Namsan Hill, the heart of the capital. Kim chose this spot specifically for the GPSH because it was 'the best place in the centre of Pyongyang' (1997: 16). Indeed, Namsan Hill remains one of the most important neighbourhoods in the country because it is the national government district, the power centre of North Korean communism. The library sits at the head of Kim Il-Sung square, the thirty-seventh-largest square in the world – which hosts the country's national events. The building has served as a backdrop to the speeches of Kim Il-Sung, Kim Jong-Il and Kim Jong-Un. It features prominently in military and nuclear weapons parades and carefully choreographed spectacles celebrating national holidays. Sitting on either side of the library is the Central Committee building of the WPK, in addition to the Ministry of External Economic Relations. On the other side of Kim Il-Sung Square and the Taedong River stands the Juche Tower, the physical manifestation of Kim Il-Sung's unique Marxist-inspired philosophy. The placement of the GPSH and the Juche Tower across from each other symbolises the close bond between the people and the Juche idea. Indeed, the aim was that 'the people would study the Juche idea looking at the tower from the study house' (FLPH 2006: 171). The GPSH is therefore far more than a prominent feature of the capital. It is an icon of the nation, Juche communism and the 'Eternal President' himself (Kosciejew 2009a: 169).

Kim Il-Sung also dictated the design of the GPSH. Some architects wanted to build it in a modern style. Kim rejected this and called for it to be built in Korean style so that 'all the city acquired a clearly Korean tint' (Kim Jong-Il 2006: 187, 141). The party also drew up a variety of plans for the GPSH and exhibited them in the People's Palace of Culture for the masses' criticisms. People from all sections of the population in Pyongyang participated, and according to Kim Jong-Il, they all said that Korean style was the best. 'This convinced the architects more clearly of the validity of the great leaders plan' (Kim Jong-Il 2006: 261). Kim Jong-Il instructed that the original scale be reduced to be harmonious with the surroundings. He stressed that the standard for comparison in scale could not be the size of foreign libraries but matching the size of Kim Il-Sung Square and the buildings on either side when viewed from the square. 'The idea was a flash of inspiration to the planners, who had been groping about, and they finally came up with the design and reduced the scale'. The project was completed in a year and nine months (FLPH 2006: 176).

Standing atop the Gardens of Namsam Hill, the GPSH 'resembles an ancient Korean palace with grand staircases, sweeping balconies, marble columns and green tiled pagoda-style roofs' (Kosciejew 2009a: 167). Kim Jong-Il described the GPSH as a 'great monumental structure, with socialist content in national form', 'a masterpiece by world standards'. It resembles 'a picture of a happy hen sheltering her chickens under her wings on a green lawn on a sunny spring day'. The GPSH was created 'through a concentrated reflection of the requirements of the spirits of the age of Juche, our peoples noble and beautiful sentiments, their political and moral qualities, and the advantages of the socialist system of our style'. It made 'great contributions to the ideological and emotional education of our people' and produced 'a deep aesthetic effect on them' (Kim Jong-Il 2006: 141, 204, 238).

Kim Il-Sung described the GPSH as 'both a correspondence university and an important centre for making the whole of society intellectually-proficient' (1991: 95). Besides providing a fount of knowledge for the labouring masses, he thought it would be particularly useful in 're-educating' the scientists and technicians who had graduated long ago and lagged behind recent discoveries and those who studied abroad but had a poor grasp of the language. The GPSH was the ideal location for re-educating these elements because it contained not only numerous scientific and technical books but also many translators capable of translating foreign scientific and technical books, as well as well-qualified lecturers (1995: 297–298).

Kim Il-Sung advised scientists to spend short stints at the GPSH whilst on the job rather than study there exclusively for long periods. Likewise, he encouraged the technicians working in factories and enterprises to study for one or two months at the GPSH before returning to their jobs. They could then return once they encountered difficulties at work. As he put it, 'the re-education of the scientists and technicians must be conducted in such a way as to allow them to study according to their needs and to broaden their expertise' (1995: 298).

Some officials thought that scientists and technicians from outside Pyongyang could not make good use of the Study House, since there were no hotels nearby when it was first constructed. They requested that hotels be constructed as soon as possible. Kim Il-Sung was having none of it. If scientists and technicians were enthusiastic for study, he argued, then they would come to study at the GPSH anyway, by 'staying in other people[']s houses. Our officials are so accustomed to working and living in ideal conditions that they behave like rich men's sons' (1996: 40).

Kim Il-Sung also called on party cadres and government officials to study there once a week. Doing so would enable them to expand their own mental horizons and thereby ensure that they were capable of leading the educational, cultural and ideological development of the people (1995: 298).

Kim Il-Sung viewed the GPSH as the crown jewel of the North Korean socialist library system. It symbolised the high cultural level of the nation, its intellectual proficiency and its 'people-centred' essence. Kim had these points in mind when he said:

> The Grand Peoples Study House is a monumental creation of which we can be proud before the entire world; it is one of our peoples' precious and most treasured possessions. It is not a simple library but an edifice of science and education, just like a university.
>
> (1991: 379–380)

These claims were justified. The GPSH is a truly awesome site. It covers a total floor space of 100,000 square metres and consists of 10 buildings with 10 stories. It can house 30 million books and has more than 600 rooms, including 23 reading rooms with 6000 seats, 14 lecture rooms, several information rooms and question-and-answer rooms. Today, its operation is fully computerised, and the lecture and information rooms are equipped with computers, video players, projectors and slide projectors. The books demanded by readers are automatically conveyed to the book-lending stands. Visitors are given information, question and answers and recorded and video lectures, in addition to general ones. Lectures are arranged on new scientific and technological problems, lectures on scientific theory and scientific and technological short courses are organised on a regular basis. Interactive lectures are delivered through the real-time exchange of images, sounds and letters. Ten to 12,000 students and working people visit every day (Om Hyang Sim 2017: 13–14). Among its 1000 staff, there are 400 librarians, 200 translators and more than 200 lecturers, including people with academic degrees. Besides this, there are hundreds of part-time lecturers. The house also maintains material exchange and international loan work with more than 100 countries on five continents and conducts library service and information activities for the capital and the entire country:

> Therefore, the Grand People's Study House is not merely a library which loans reading books or materials, but a correspondence course university, scientific and educational institution and a central base for the intellectualisation of society. It helps the working people including scientists, technicians and specialists to enhance their level of knowledge, and solves the knotty problems in scientific research work and informs the people about development trends in world science and technology.
>
> (Li Yong Rip 1996: 24–25)

Kim Il-Sung is an omnipresent figure in the GPSH. Upon entering the library, visitors are greeted with a colossal stature of the Eternal President. 'Lit by retro-soviet chandeliers and framed by Romanesque columns, the white marble statue sits atop an imposing throne, with a mural backdrop of the country's revered Mount Paekdu'. Both 'the statue and backdrop create a strong impression of the power and majesty of Kim Il-Sung'. Not only does the throne show his unquestioned authority. 'The scene of Mount Paekdu reinforces the idea that the man *is* North Korea and therefore a significant part of the national identity'. Visitors cannot simply wander by this imposing scene. 'All individuals who enter the GPSH must pay their respects to the Eternal President by bowing. Interacting with the statue in this way demonstrates one[']s acknowledgement of and respect for Kim Il-Sung's gift of libraries and education to the North Korean people'. The Eternal President does not just greet visitors at the entrance. He watches over patrons and staff in every section of the building. Along with images of Kim Jong-Il, his portrait is displayed prominently in 'every reading room, lecture hall, office, and atrium. While patrons read, write and study, Kim Il-Sung observes them. His portraits gaze over the library space, connecting visitors to his greatness and reminding visitors of their constant surveillance' (Kosciejew 2009b: 208). There is even a reading room devoted entirely to the 'works of President Kim Il-Sung and books on his greatness'.

Kim Il-Sung's presence can be felt not only in the GPSH. His image is displayed in every library across the country. The role of the GPSH in entrenching this national cult of the personality – as well as the role played by all libraries – cannot be overstated (Kosciejew 2009b: 208).

North Korean public libraries in comparative perspective

In its general national structure, North Korea's public library service is similar to the Marxist-Leninist model. Besides having a national library in the nation's capital, there is a 'well organised state-library system at the provincial, city, and county levels in the country' (Li Yong Rip 1996: 24). But based as they are on the Juche idea, North Korea's libraries are also distinct in several ways from their Marxist-Leninist counterparts. Some of these differences have already been discussed, although it is useful, at this point, to make the main ones explicit. Doing this can help illuminate the unique characteristics of the DPRK socialist public library system.

North Korea's public libraries place a far greater emphasis on ideological work. Although Marxism-Leninism also stresses the importance of ideology in sustaining socialism, its main emphasis is on material factors, specifically the productive forces of society. In China, the most explicit example of this, the economic development of the country and the consequent improvement in living standards is, in the eyes of the party – the most important force in legitimising the political system and maintaining support for it. China's public libraries are therefore oriented towards developing the technical and scientific knowledge of the populace. Ideological education in Marxism-Leninism is of secondary importance for the libraries. On the whole, the same is true for Cuba, Vietnam and Laos. In these countries, the public libraries prioritise economic development over ideological development.

In North Korea, the opposite is the case. The Juche idea prioritises ideology over everything else. For Juche, unlike Marxism-Leninism, the socialist order is based above all on the ideological education of the masses, not a high level of economic development. In North Korea, therefore, the public libraries focus much more upon imbuing the masses with the Juche idea. The rationale is that if everyone commits themselves steadfastly to this idea, then the country will be able to survive the most difficult economic hardships. In the DPRK, the public libraries, like all the other education institutions, are primarily ideological. Every citizen is expected to go to the library and read the works of Kim Il-Sung, Kim Jong-Il and the party so as to develop their ideological consciousness and loyalty to the regime. The relative importance of technology and science has been stressed more in recent years, particularly since Kim Jong-Un took power. Nevertheless, ideological work remains at the core of North Korean cultural life, including the libraries.

A second difference between North Korean and Marxist-Leninist public libraries concerns the aim and scope of their ideological functions. Marxism-Leninism prides itself on being a critically minded science. It encourages people not to adopt a dogmatic outlook but a critical, creative and independent one. As such, the public libraries in the Marxist-Leninist countries do not try to mould people's thoughts, ideas or beliefs in the same way. On the contrary, they strive to meet the diverse needs of the patrons and try to give them the resources to pursue their own goals. Although Marxist-Leninist public libraries do contribute to the creation of new communist individuals, they do not want these individuals to be ideologically homogeneous in outlook. A general commitment to socialism and communism is endorsed, but beyond that, the Marxist-Leninist libraries encourage people to pursue whatever activities and ideas they like.

North Korea is a different story. The DPRK is committed to the creation of a 'Monolithic Ideological System', one in which the entire population is of one mind. Everyone must subscribe to the same basic beliefs, and this means that they must not only support socialism and communism. They must also have identical views on society, culture, philosophy, history, ethics and other such subjects. There is no room for diversity in ideas. There is no room for heterogeneity in thought. The entire nation – the party, the leader and the masses – must be a single 'socio-political organism'. It must have one brain and outlook. In short, there must be *total unity*. As such, North Korea's public libraries do not attempt to encourage diverse beliefs and critically minded citizens. They do not want to create independent free-thinking individuals. They instead strive to consolidate the Monolithic Ideological System, the ideological unity of the nation. North Korea's libraries maintain this unity by carefully selecting the range of books and information material available to the people. Publications that feature ideas contrary to the monolithic ideology are prohibited or censored. As for the internet, North Korean citizens have no access to the World Wide Web. They can only access the DPRK's own internal intranet, the content of which is, of course, completely controlled by the state. As such, when public library patrons use the computers in the libraries, all the information they access will contribute to the development of a single monolithic consciousness.

Bourgeois scholars invariably interpret this public library function as one that helps destroy individual freedom. North Koreans would disagree. Their country has a centuries-old Confucian tradition of prioritising the collective over the individual, group harmony over individual anarchy. For North Koreans, individual freedom does not mean the individual's ability to do what they like but the collective's ability to maintain its unity and decide its destiny. The individual can be free only by becoming part of the collective, both materially and ideologically. Insofar as the public libraries contribute to the solidification of collective unity, they serve this distinctly Korean conception of freedom.

North Korean and Marxist-Leninist public libraries have differing degrees of autonomy. Both kinds are owned and controlled by the state, which sets their general principles of organisation and long-term development. This centralisation limits the autonomy and independence of each library. Nevertheless, the Marxist-Leninist public libraries do have some autonomy. They do have some independence. They are able, for instance, to organise their own events, functions and services in accordance with the specific needs of their local communities. The masses can also make requests that the public libraries, within reason, can strive to implement so long as they are in accordance with the state plan.

This is not the case in North Korea. Since the Juche idea emphasises the necessity of ideological training and total ideological unity, the state exerts direct control over virtually every aspect of cultural life. This is how it has managed to keep a far more monolithic and homogeneous culture since its inception. The public libraries are no exception. The state decides all their functions from the national to the local village level. This has given the DPRK's public libraries a degree of uniformity unmatched anywhere else in the world. They all feature more or less the same characteristics, and there is very little variation between them. This means that like the people, state and party, the public libraries look and operate as a single 'organism'.

A fourth distinctive feature of North Korea's public library system is its autarkic character. Marxist-Leninist public libraries are not isolated. They feature extensive international cooperation with foreign bourgeois libraries. They exchange books, information and resources, in addition to maintaining frequent contact and communications. By contrast, a key doctrine of North Korea's Juche idea is *national self-reliance*. According to this doctrine, which permeates every aspect of the country, the DPRK must rely as much as it can upon its own resources and strive to become a self-sustaining, self-sufficient, independent nation. Therefore, with the GPSH as a notable exception, the public libraries have minimal contact with foreign libraries. The system is for the most part self-contained within the country's borders. Although the public libraries within the country exchange books, information and the like amongst each other, they communicate little with libraries outside the country. Most of North Korea's books are published internally, by its state publishing houses. In comparison to the Marxist-Leninist nations, the libraries contain far fewer foreign-published books.

Last but not least, North Korea's public libraries are distinguished by their role in maintaining the Kim family dynasty. In the Marxist-Leninist countries, the leading force of society is the party of the working class. Although every party has a leader, this leader is never elevated above the party itself. This fact is reflected in the public libraries. In Cuba, China, Vietnam and Laos, the public libraries in their activities strive to make the population loyal to the party.

In North Korea, by contrast, the party leader is championed as the most powerful ruling force of the country, and the party comes in second. It has already been shown that portraits of Kim Il-Sung and Kim Jong-Il feature in virtually every room of the GPSH. This is true for the nation's libraries more generally. A key function of North Korea's public libraries is to enhance the population's loyalty to and love for the 'Great Leader'. They help maintain the old Confucian ideal of 'filial piety', that is devotion and obedience to one's parents – except that the parents in North Korea are not only the biological ones but also the 'fatherly leader' Kim Il-Sung. Every public library features Kim's voluminous works, often in a special dedicated section, and every citizen is obliged to regularly visit and read these works, as part of the country's slogan that people must constantly study whilst working. Public librarians must also show complete devotion to the leader. They all wear pins with pictures of Kim Il-Sung and Kim Jong-Il. Readers are expected to read and learn not only for their own sakes but also in the service of the Great Leader.

Like their Marxist-Leninist counterparts, North Korean public libraries have encountered several setbacks in their growth. The DPRK is a poor nation that suffers from shortages in vital foodstuffs and resources. As such, the public libraries in some of the country's more deprived areas are still under-developed and in need of more books, more advanced technology and better facilities. Contrary to the views of bourgeois commentators, North Korea's Juche ideology is *not* to blame for this state of affairs. The forces of imperialism are to blame. The fact of the matter is that since the country was born, the imperialist nations have subjected it to international economic sanctions more restrictive than any other country. The DPRK has been starved of resources, and that is why Juche promotes economic self-sufficiency. This policy was not therefore an arbitrary one. It emerged as a matter of necessity. If the international economic sanctions on North Korea were lifted even slightly, then the country would be able to accelerate the expansion of its socialist public library system.

Conclusion

This chapter sought to provide a deeper insight into North Korean public libraries and the role they play in society. The aim was to showcase the rich diversity of Marxist-Leninist library systems and to also draw some lessons for constructing the Vanguard library. Kim Il-Sung argued that libraries are significant for four reasons. First, they aid the development of equality. They help the working masses, who cannot always afford books, to educate and thereby empower themselves. Second, public libraries are instruments of political indoctrination. They imbue the masses with the Juche idea and maintain ideological unity in the country. Third, libraries are physical manifestations of cultural development. They embody the high cultural level of a country, which is an especially important indicator for socialist states. Fourth, libraries are manifestations of self-reliance. They allow the socialist nation to educate its people by itself and solve its own problems.

Finally, and most important, the core principle of the Juche philosophy is that socialism can be built in one country without relying on other countries for help. By extension, the DPRK has proved that a socialist public library system can be developed *at any time and any place, even when the objective conditions are not ideal*, so long as the masses and librarians are armed with the correct theory and leadership. To word the same point differently, the masses can transform *any* unfavourable conditions for socialist library construction into favourable conditions so long as they have a working-class outlook and leadership. To be sure, this principle also underlies the Marxist-Leninist public library systems. They, too, affirm the possibility of building a socialist library system in one country through the workers' own efforts. At the same time, however, the Marxist-Leninist countries also tend to emphasise the significance of the objective conditions in facilitating this process. In doing so, they tend to downplay the significance of the subjective factor, the human will. Kim Il-Sung was the first Marxist-Leninist to emphasise that the masses themselves can *create* the necessary objective conditions for socialist public libraries. They can build public libraries under *any circumstances, so long as they retain the revolutionary outlook of the fighting working class*. This is the core Juche principle motivating North Korea's approach to public library organisation. This is also a core tenet of the Vanguard public library, which is examined next.

Note

1 Unless otherwise stated, all in-text references are to Kim Il-Sung.

References

FLPH (Foreign Languages Publishing House) (2001) *Kim Il-Sung: Condensed Biography*. Pyongyang: Foreign Languages Publishing House.

—— (2006) *Kim Jong-Il: Biography*, Vol. 2. Pyongyang: Foreign Languages Publishing House.

Kim Il-Sung (1980a) *Works*, Vol. 2. Pyongyang: Foreign Languages Publishing House.

—— (1980b) *Works*, Vol. 3. Pyongyang: Foreign Languages Publishing House.
—— (1981a) *Works*, Vol. 4. Pyongyang: Foreign Languages Publishing House.
—— (1981b) *Works*, Vol. 8. Pyongyang: Foreign Languages Publishing House.
—— (1982) *Works*, Vol. 9. Pyongyang: Foreign Languages Publishing House.
—— (1985a) *Works*, Vol. 23. Pyongyang: Foreign Languages Publishing House.
—— (1985b) *Works*, Vol. 24. Pyongyang: Foreign Languages Publishing House.
—— (1985c) *Works*, Vol. 21. Pyongyang: Foreign Languages Publishing House.
—— (1986a) *Works*, Vol. 28. Pyongyang: Foreign Languages Publishing House.
—— (1986b) *Works*, Vol. 25. Pyongyang: Foreign Languages Publishing House.
—— (1987) *Works*, Vol. 29. Pyongyang: Foreign Languages Publishing House.
—— (1988) *Works*, Vol. 32. Pyongyang: Foreign Languages Publishing House.
—— (1989) *Works*, Vol. 35. Pyongyang: Foreign Languages Publishing House.
—— (1991) *Works*, Vol. 37. Pyongyang: Foreign Languages Publishing House.
—— (1993) *Works*, Vol. 38. Pyongyang: Foreign Languages Publishing House.
—— (1994a) *Reminisces: With the Century*, Vol. 1. Pyongyang: Foreign Languages Publishing House.
—— (1994b) *Reminisces: With the Century*, Vol. 2. Pyongyang: Foreign Languages Publishing House.
—— (1995) *Works*, Vol. 39. Pyongyang: Foreign Languages Publishing House.
—— (1996) *Works*, Vol. 41. Pyongyang: Foreign Languages Publishing House.
—— (1997) *Works*, Vol. 42. Pyongyang: Foreign Languages Publishing House.
—— (1999) *Works*, Vol. 44. Pyongyang: Foreign Languages Publishing House.

Kim Jong-Il (2006) *Selected Works*, Vol. 11. Pyongyang: Foreign Languages Publishing House.
—— (2014) *Selected Works*, Vol. 14. Pyongyang: Foreign Languages Publishing House.
Kosciejew, M. (2009a) 'Inside an Axis of Evil Library: A First-Hand Account of the North Korean Dear Leader's Library System Part One', *Feliciter*, 55/4: 167–170.
—— (2009b). 'Inside an Axis of Evil Library: A First-Hand Account of the North Korean Dear Leader's Library System Part Two', *Feliciter*, 55/5: 207–209.
Li Yong Rip (1996) 'Scientific and Technical Information Activities in the Democratic Peoples Republic of Korea', in G. Harris and R. Creamer (eds.) *Better Read Than Dead: Libraries in Cuba, China, North Korea and Vietnam*. Link/ISC Conference Proceedings 16th March 1996, VSO, Putney, London, UK, Special Issue of "Link-Up", Vol. 8, No. 1.
Om Hyang Sim (2017) *Culture: Understanding Korea Series, No. 6*. Pyongyang: Foreign Languages Publishing House.

5 The Vanguard library

In this chapter, we explore why a Vanguard library is necessary and how it can exist in both capitalist and socialist societies. We give examples of the Vanguard library under both systems, drawing on the experience of the miners' libraries in South Wales in the early twentieth century and the transformation of public libraries after the triumph of the revolution in Cuba in 1959. We will also give details of the key elements of a Vanguard library, from its strategy and structures to its systems and organisational culture. The purpose of doing this is to provide a road map and a blueprint for how a Vanguard library can be constructed. It is possible to lay down the foundations of a Vanguard library regardless of the prevailing economic, political and social environment. As Marxists, we believe that not only must we understand the world, but we must also seek to change it. So this chapter is a call to action, a call to build a Vanguard library that can meet the needs of the working class.

What is the Vanguard library, and why do we need it?

The essence of Vanguardism is that the masses can free themselves only if they are led by a class-conscious professional organisation armed with Marxist theory. Vanguardism emphasises the importance of leadership in undertaking revolutionary change (Gordon-Nesbitt 2015: 106–107). This means that the leading force of progressive change in the public library should be a Marxist vanguard that can harness the spontaneous forces of the patrons and staff to meet the needs of the working class. Whereas Marx had expected false consciousness to be shed spontaneously when capitalism was overturned through mass action, Lenin's vanguardist approach implied that revolutionary consciousness would need to be both stimulated and sustained in the broader populace. The vanguard role attributed by Lenin to the party and its intellectuals manifested itself in Cuba, and a shared commitment to change established a necessary link between political and artistic vanguards, in service of the revolution. Artists were encouraged to take cultural weapons of the highest quality to the people. They were also encouraged to study Marxism not as a political act but as an artistic one as well. Echoing Stalin's evocation of writers as 'engineers of the human soul', the National Council of Culture insisted that artists and writers should be '[c]apable of representing in their work not only objective reality but also reality in its revolutionary development, helping it in its important task of transforming old ways of thinking and lapsed ideas, educating workers in the spirit of socialism' (National Council of Culture 1963: 2).

It was observed that in Cuba the majority of vanguard artists were also at the political vanguard:

> The political vanguard is a minority but by no means minor, being the cutting edge of a class. The artistic vanguard, in a similar way, if it really is a vanguard, is not a minority . . . but the cutting edge of a coalition which, sooner or later, is going to embrace the consequences of the vanguard.
>
> (Retamar 1966: 284)

It was also observed that, much quicker than European socialist countries, the political and aesthetic vanguards in Cuba had reached a state in which they could fertilise one another. Whereas Celaya had made the vanguardist assertion that '[t]he intellectual is obliged to raise themselves up to the people and to walk a path in front of them' (Cuban Book Institute 1968: unpaginated), Benedetti suggested a reciprocal process in which

> The man of action should be a 'trail blazer' of the intellectual and vice versa. That is, in the dynamic aspect of the Revolution, the man of action should be the vanguard for the intellectual and, in the sphere of art, of thought, of scientific research, the intellectual should be the vanguard for the man of action.
>
> (1968: 31)

The challenge in all socialist countries was to ensure that the political and artistic vanguards were not divorced from each other. The Cuban Revolution ended this dichotomy. The artist was regarded as a permanent rebel, and the objectives of vanguard art were to change man and society at the same time, using the weapons of imagination and critique. Uniting both vanguards, it was argued that '[e]ducation, productive work and, above all, the defence of the Revolution, which is the defence of culture, are tasks common to all revolutionaries' (Cuban Book Institute 1968: unpaginated). Fidel Castro said that he fully expected the imperialists to regard the 1968 Cultural

Congress of Havana, which was a pivotal moment in the history of Cuban cultural development, to be a 'Vietnam in the field of culture', with intellectual workers taking increasingly militant positions. Cultural work had been invoked by intellectuals as the ideological corollary of armed struggle. The revolutionary intellectual had to direct their work towards eradicating the vestiges of the old society that persist in the transition period from capitalism to socialism. Creative intellectuals were incited to take their work to the people in an open and dialogical way (Freire 1979). Culture was recognised as both intrinsically valuable and inherently revolutionary. Mao-Tse-Tung called this a 'proletarian revolutionary utilitarian' approach to art:

> Literature and art are subordinate to politics, but in their turn exert a great influence on politics. Revolutionary literature and art are part of the whole revolutionary cause, they are cogs and wheels in it, and though in comparison with certain other and more important parts they may be less significant and less urgent and may occupy a secondary position, nevertheless, they are indispensable cogs and wheels in the whole machine, an indispensable part of the entire revolutionary cause. If we had no literature and art even in the broadest and most ordinary sense, we could not carry on the revolutionary movement and win victory. Failure to recognize that is wrong.
>
> (1991: 866)

As Aneurin Bevan pointed out, '[s]ocial institutions are what they do, not necessarily what we say they do. It is the verb that matters, not the noun' (1952: 13). In capitalist countries, public libraries are what they do – they serve the interests of the minority bourgeois class – rather than what they say they do, which is to be neutral, apolitical, democratic and open to all. As we demonstrated in Chapter 2, public libraries serve a middle-class interest and are inherently undemocratic. By substituting the term *public* with *vanguard*, we align what the Vanguard library does with what we say it does.

We have previously argued that the public library is a part of the ideological superstructure that is shaped and determined by the economic base of a society at any given stage in its development (Pateman and Pateman 2019). This suggests that the public library is not a static institution but one that evolves in response to changes to the economic system. Consequently, the public library in a capitalist economic system is different to a public library in a socialist system which, in turn, is different to a public library in a communist system. It is therefore possible to align the development of the public library with different periods of material and historical development. During the capitalist period of development, for example, the public library typically takes on the form of the Traditional library. The strategy, structures, systems and ideology of this library advance the interests of the bourgeoisie. During the socialist period of development, the Traditional library evolves into the Community-Led library which advances the interests of the proletariat. The highest stage of development of the public library takes place under communism, when class differences have disappeared and the Community-Led library evolves into the Needs-Based library. The role of the Vanguard library is to lead the evolution of the public library from one period of historical and material development to the next stage.

The Vanguard library can exist under capitalism. This is so because capitalism is a contradictory mode of production, one that creates the seeds of socialism *and* communism within itself. This fact is also consistent with the concept of socialism in one country. On one hand, Marxism asserts that socialism can be built in one country. On the other hand, it asserts that a country can safeguard its socialist achievements (i.e. achieve a final victory) only once there has been a worldwide revolution. Likewise, the Vanguard public library can establish itself in a capitalist country, although it can secure its achievements only after the transition to socialism. The Traditional library will wither under socialism, and the Community-Led library will become the Vanguard library. Similarly, the Community-Led library will wither in the communist period, and the Needs-Based library will become the Vanguard library. In each material and historical period of development, the Vanguard library leads the transformation process from one type of public library to another. This is consistent with the concept of the permanent revolution which states that organisations should constantly revolutionise (i.e. change) themselves in order to maintain the achievements of the revolution and stay in tune with wider developments. If the Vanguard library wishes to remain relevant, popular, meaningful and useful to the masses, it must constantly revolutionise its practices.

The Vanguard library plays a pedagogical role during each phase of material and historical development. The purpose of this education is to develop the class consciousness of the proletariat. In the capitalist period, this means providing the working class with the tools they need to engage in the class struggle. Class oppression under capitalism is sometimes very obvious, but it can also be very subtle and hidden, particularly under neo-liberalism, which is the current and most advanced stage of capitalist development. Neo-liberal ideology, which permeates and controls the mass media, seeks to convince the working class that capitalism is good for them. The Vanguard library can remove this veil from the eyes of the working class and reveal the true nature of capitalist society – that the proletariat (the oppressed) is dominated and exploited by the bourgeoisie (the oppressor). Paulo Freire (1979) suggests that working-class consciousness can be developed by taking what he calls a dialogical approach. The Vanguard library does not assume that it can simply 'bank' class consciousness into the empty heads of the working class. The Vanguard library understands that the starting point has to be the lived experience and material conditions of the proletariat, because these are what shape and determine class consciousness. This dialogical approach was used in Cuba to develop 'the new socialist man' (Guevara 1965).

The role of the Vanguard library is consistent with the concept of cultural revolution. According to Marxism, the material transformation of society does not immediately eradicate old ideas. These have relative autonomy from the economic base and can exist long after this base has been transformed. A cultural revolution is a concerted mass effort to eradicate these old ideas. It involves a dialectical interplay of leadership and mass spontaneity. In order for the Vanguard library to preserve the achievements of its material changes (e.g. changes in strategies, structures and systems), it must undertake cultural revolutions.

In order to better explain the role of the Vanguard library during these different periods of material and historical development, we give some examples of how the Vanguard library operates within capitalist and socialist) societies. We are not able to give any examples of how the Vanguard library operates under a communist economic system because no society has yet reached this stage of development.

The Vanguard library under capitalism

> The library open to all is no good for the workers for many reasons. In library work particular attention is required in respect to the workers, as most of them are not trained readers, and hence they are the most difficult and most important customers. The literature which is the pabulum of our bourgeois reader is more often than not unsuitable for the worker, it contains much that does not interest him, much that is not within his reach and, in the final account, is superfluous and unnecessary. To select the right book for him one must know his psychology, which one can study only by working individually with him. The American library teaches that one must take into account the psychology of the individual reader, demands individualization of reading. But individualization is insufficient and unfeasible unless one takes into account class psychology, which American libraries refuse to recognise. One must not only take class psychology into account, one must also study it, and in one's work create the new core of the modern library.
> (Dobler 1983: 64)

The public library as a cultural category under the capitalist economic system is mostly located in the private market and has a commodity character that exempts them from playing a social role. In the UK, for example, since 1979, there has been a recession of the state from the funding arena in favour of private enterprise and instrumental approaches. Culture is largely the domain of the bourgeoisie both in terms of production and consumption. Culture is an ideological product of capitalism and seeks to make a profit for the individual rather than providing a collective benefit for the whole of society.

One of the best examples of the Vanguard library under capitalism is the miners' libraries that operated at pit heads across the South Wales coalfield of the UK in the 1920s and 1930s. While these were not 'public libraries' in the generally accepted use of the term (funded and operated by local government), they were 'public' libraries in the true sense of the term in that they were owned and operated by the working class: 'The miners' institutes of South Wales were one of the greatest networks of cultural institutions created by working people anywhere in the world' (Rose 2002: 237).

Many of the Welsh miners' libraries began in the nineteenth century, at first under middle-class patronage. Victorian colliers authorised deductions from the miners' wages to pay for their children's education, but when school fees were abolished in 1891, this money was redirected towards the miner's institutes. As the miners themselves covered the ongoing expenses, they controlled the libraries. By 1934, there were more than 100 miner's libraries in the Welsh coalfields, with an average collection of about 3000 books. In mid-Rhondda, there were 40,000 books a month in circulation from four libraries. The pride of the movement was the Tredegar Workmen's Institute which by the Second World War was circulating 100,000 books a year. It was in a miners' library that many young miners first heard the names of economists and philosophers such as Einstein, Spencer, Darwin and Marx: 'At a street corner in Tony Pandy I heard two young miners discussing Einstein's *Theory of Relativity*. I know this was exceptional, but it is significant and it is true' (Morton 1932: 247)

One young miner joined the library committee of the Miners' Institute in Maesteg, made friends with the librarian, and advised him on acquisitions: 'Thus he could read all the books he wanted: Marx, Smith, Ricardo, Mill, Marshall, economic and trade union history, Fabian essays, Thomas Hardy, Meredith, Kipling and Dickens' (Rose 2002: 240). Marxists were often members of the library book selection committee. The committee at Tredegar was headed by Aneurin Bevan:

> Tredegar Workmen's Library was unusually well stocked with books of all kinds. . . . I was especially fortunate in the quality of the library which had been built up by the pennies of the miners and given its distinctive quality by a small band of extraordinary men, themselves miners and self educated. They made available to us both the orthodox

economists and philosophers, and the Marxist source books, and thus showed a more receptive attitude and less bigotry than many of our school and college libraries at that time.

(1952: 17–19)

What Bevan called 'a small band of extraordinary men' were the advanced guard, or vanguard, of the miners. These autodidacts combined their lived experience and Marxist theory to form a trained and disciplined cadre of Vanguard library workers. They had an acute class consciousness that guided all their actions. Everything they did was in the interest of the working class. Their library collections often contained the complete works of Marx, Engels and Lenin. Their intention was to raise the class consciousness of the miners, and there was no better place to do so than in the miners' institute which was located at the pit head, where they laboured for long hours underground in indescribable conditions. After a day's work, they could connect their working lives with the works of Marx and others to understand how their material conditions were shaped and determined by the underlying economic system. This gave them the tools to engage in the class struggle; indeed, they were often in the front line of that struggle. The Vanguard library gave them the weapons with which to wage that battle.

As Aneurin Bevan suggests, the political education he received at Tredegar Workmen's Library was different to that which he could have expected from other types of libraries, including the local public library. The book collections of the miners' libraries – unlike those of public libraries – offered a profile of working-class reading preferences uncontaminated by middle-class cultural hegemony. The library at Tylorstown Workmen's Institute, for example, included novels by Jack London (*White Fang, The Iron Heel*), George Orwell (*The Road to Wigan Pier*) and D. H. Lawrence (*Sons and Lovers, Women in Love*); the plays of George Bernard Shaw; and the works of Marx (*Das Kapital, Critique of the Gotha Program*) and Engels (*Origin of the Family*). Tredegar Workmen's Library provided the complete works of Lenin:

> The village of Mardy was a 'little Moscow' where in 1933 ninety colliers were studying the proletarian philosopher Joseph Dietzgen at the Miners' Institute. . . . As one collier explained, "The conveyor face down the Number 2 Pit was a university" where Darwin, Marx, Paine . . . were debated.
>
> (Rose 2002: 249)

The miners' libraries reflected working-class culture and interests and were heavily used by the proletariat. The same cannot be said of the public libraries in mining communities which were visited by just 20 per cent of the local people, and a mere 6 per cent regularly borrowed materials. The miners' libraries were particularly well used during periods of economic depression and unemployment. Between 1920 and 1928, the Cwmaman Workmen's Institute saw book borrowing double from 14,966 to 31,054. One library in Ynyshir was used by 300 out-of-work miners who borrowed a total of 500 books a week, an average of 86 books per year. Those who were unemployed for long periods could read several hundred books. Out-of-work men commonly and quite plausibly claimed to read three or four books a week. The reading habits of these unemployed men reflected their material conditions. At the Markham Miners' Library, men borrowed the literature of political commitment: Upton Sinclair's *Oil*, Ralph Bates's *Lean Men*, Robert Tresswell's *The Ragged Trousered Philanthropists*, Mikhail Sholokhov's *Quiet Flows the Don* and the social realism of Feodor Gladkov's *Cement*. They also borrowed Engels's *The Origin of the Family* and works by proletarian intellectuals like T. A. Jackson, Bert Coombes, W. H. Davies, Willie Gallacher and Joseph Dietzgen. During periods of unemployment, the miner's libraries sharpened the class consciousness of the proletariat; the role of the public library at these times, on the other hand, was to divert and distract the working class in an attempt to defuse some of the class tensions and political pressure that built up within the capitalist system.

The Vanguard library under socialism

> The future of Cuban culture is determined not merely by advances in specifically cultural fields but also by the parallel economic and social development and the building of a socialist society. The march towards communism is in itself a movement towards the reign of culture, towards the conversion of every aspect of human life into an aesthetic experience. The premises of this evolution are: (a) the elimination of the class struggle and an all-round approach to education and culture thanks to which all human beings can become recipients and creators of art; (b) the dissemination of general education and artistic education; (c) the constant growth of artistic output and aesthetic needs; and (d) the emergence of aesthetic behaviour as a higher form of relationship between man and nature, between the individual and society.
>
> (Sarusky and Mosquera 1979: 20)

> [This] requires an understanding of Marxism as a philosophy of praxis; more precisely of a praxis which aims to transform human reality radically (on a concrete, historical level, to transform capitalist society) so as to establish a society in which humanity can give free reign to its essential powers, frustrated, denied, postponed and emasculated for so long. This understanding of Marxism as the true humanism, as the radical transformation of humanity on all planes, fulfills Marx's aspiration. Aesthetics cannot

> be alien to this humanist Marxism, since . . . it is an essential dimension of human existence.
>
> (Sanchez Vasquez 1973: 10)

These statements perfectly illustrate the Marxist-humanist attitude to culture. Central to this is the idea that the revolution would bring about positive changes in the evolution of humanity and that contact with culture would help pave the way for this transformation. The enjoyment of culture in Cuba was made available to all as part of the collective project of creating a happier individual and social consciousness:

> Marxist-humanist cultural policy, as it has been formulated in Cuba is underwritten by the conviction that those taking up mental labour may emerge from any sector in society. This democratising impulse entails that passive spectatorship of, and active engagement in, creative production are necessary to human fulfilment. In regard to spectatorship, culture was immediately conceived as the patrimony of an entire population, with cultural works from previous eras acknowledged to provide glimpses of humanity's evolution, making them worthy of preservation.
>
> (Gordon-Nesbitt 2015: 328)

In *The German Ideology*, Marx and Engels gave specific attention to the position of the artist within capitalist society. They concluded that artists were inextricably linked to their socio-economic surroundings. In the *Grundrisse*, Marx found that the artefacts of Greek culture continued to provide aesthetic pleasure long after their production. Engels popularised the idea that art, in general, had a part to play in the construction of socialism. Both Marx and Engels exempted art and literature from being explicitly ideological and dissociated the ideology of an artwork from that of its producer. Lenin pointed out that

> [f]ar from rejecting the most valuable achievements of the bourgeois epoch, Marxism, in the contrary, has assimilated and reshaped the more valuable elements accumulated in the course of more than two thousand years of development of human thought and culture.
>
> (1960: 79–80)

Acknowledging Lenin's ideas about the inextricable relationship between creative production and class struggle, the Provincial Council of Culture declared that

[a]rtistic creation cannot remain at the margins of the class struggle ... for the simple reason that all writers and artists ... express and bring together in their work the interests of one or other of the classes.

(1961: 3)

Similarly, the Cuban Book Institute suggested that '[c]ulture, like education, is not, nor can it be, either impartial or apolitical. It is a social and historical phenomenon conditioned by the needs of social classes and their struggles and interests throughout time' (1971: unpaginated). In turn, Cuban creative intellectuals acknowledged that '[t]he carrier of words is also a carrier of a determined ideological content, of a determined vision of the world, of a determined class position' (Dalton et al. 1969: 20). Elaborating on the humanistic attributes of Marxism in relation to culture, Adolfo Sanchez Vazquez noted that

[b]ecause of its class origin, its ideological character, art is an expression of the social division or gash in humanity; but because of its ability to extend a bridge between people across time and social divisions, art manifests a vocation for universality, and in a certain way prefigures that universal human destiny which will only effectively be realized in a new society, with the abolition of the material and ideological particularisms of social classes.

(1973: 24–25)

Sochor emphasised the need for both political and cultural change within the revolutionary process:

Among the problems facing revolutionary leaders, one of the most difficult is how to transform the attitudes, beliefs and customs inherited from the old society that hinder the creation of a new society. Clearly, there is no automatic change when power is seized; the population at large may have altered its expectations but not its familiar habits in work and social behaviour. Yet without cultural transformation, the building of socialism may remain an evasive goal. Even when the political opposition has been subdued and economic development has at least been launched, the cultural sphere is not easily changed. Revolution and culture are pitted against each other.

(1988: 3)

In the Cuban context, Castro said, 'Building socialism and communism is not just a matter of producing and distributing wealth but is also a matter of education and consciousness' (1994: 147). Central to ideas around expanding consciousness would be an elaboration of the new revolutionary subject or 'new man'. Gramsci had speculated about this concept, taking Lenin's original to be shorthand for new social relations. For Che Guevara, the new man was a subject motivated by class consciousness more than the promise of fiscal reward. The new man would be encouraged to achieve full, un-alienated consciousness through holistic participation in society and culture. Guevara argued that increased acculturation would be the key to both economic growth and human realisation:

> It is still necessary to deepen conscious participation, individual and collective, in all the structures of management and production, and to link this to the idea of the need for technical and ideological education, so that the individual will realise that these processes are closely inter-dependent and their advancement is parallel. In this way, the individual will reach total consciousness as a human creature, once the chains of alienation are broken. This will be translated concretely into the re-conquering of one's true nature, through liberated labour and the expression of one's own human condition through culture and art.
>
> (1965: unpaginated)

Arnold Wesker, commenting on Guevara's conception of the 'new man', observed that the Cubans '[a]re actually looking at the acquisitive and competitive nature of man as we believed it must always be and saying: he is like this only from centuries of conditioning and we are now going to completely change that conditioning' (1969: 15). Culture would prepare the ideological terrain for the transformation of society:

> Far from being mere vanguard accomplishments, then, cultural democracy and the project of socializing art within the Cuban Revolution of 1959 were in fact manifestations of the Cuban populace intervening in history and assuming an active role in national affairs.
>
> (Craven 2006: 92)

The public library as a cultural category under the socialist economic system is funded by the state, subjected to the dictatorship of the proletariat and created for the betterment of society. Within the Soviet context, Dobler observed that

> [w]ith the social overturn which our revolution brought with it, the spiritual culture of our society must also be changed. Our task is to

restructure everything in such a way as to make it easier for the new shoots of proletarian culture to sprout and grow strong.

(1983: 64)

It has been suggested that Cuba is perhaps the best example of how this was achieved in practice: 'In its totality, the experiment carried out in Cuba from 1959 onwards represents the most ambitious rethinking of cultural provision and participation from a Marxian perspective in the twentieth century' (Gordon-Nesbitt 2015).

The Cultural Policy of the Cuban Revolution is based on five key operational principles laid down by the state. According to these principles, Cuban culture

1 belongs to everyone (as both spectators and creators) rather than being limited to an elite minority;
2 should be detached from the market economy (copyright was revoked from 1967 to 1975, in a bid to provide access to the best of the world's literature, and grants for artists were implemented from 1961);
3 is a form of social production (with humanity's happiness as its end product);
4 stimulates not only social but also economic development (by increasing the cultural levels of the population in a country emerging from underdevelopment); and
5 promotes revolutionary (and hence critical) thinking.

During 1961, which became known as the Year of Education, a census was conducted which identified 985,000 illiterates in Cuba. The universities were closed, and some 250,000 urbanites (among them 100,000 students), armed with politicised teaching manuals, oil lamps and oversized pencils, were sent out into the countryside to teach the population to read (ironing out some of the inequalities that persisted between urban and rural areas, which the revolution was committed to overcoming; Gordon-Nesbitt 2015: 22). A specially designed flag was hoisted in villages to signal the eradication of illiteracy, which, within one year, dropped to just 3.7 per cent. To put this in context, the Skills for Life survey – commissioned by the UK Department for Education and Skills in 2001 – found that 5.2 million (8.8 percent) of working-age adults had lower than basic (G grade GCSE) literacy. Similarly, in 2009, the US Education Department published the findings of its National Assessment of Adult Literacy, which showed that one in seven US adults (14.3 percent) could not read anything more complicated than a children's book. Cuba is cited as having the second-highest literacy rate in the world, with the UK and US falling 44th and 45th, respectively.

The eradication of illiteracy in Cuba primed the population for informed participation in culture. In his 'Words to Intellectuals' at the National Library on 30 June 1961, Fidel Castro said:

> Just as we want a better life for the people in the material sphere, so do we want a better life for the people in a spiritual and cultural sense. And just as the Revolution is concerned with the development of the conditions and forces that will permit the people to satisfy all their material needs, so do we also want to create the conditions that will permit the people to satisfy all their cultural needs.
>
> (1962: 19)

The notion of culture as artistic creation overflowed into conceptions of culture as part of a conscious process of construction which had human growth as its ultimate purpose. At the same time, intellectuals had a duty to defend and develop the revolution:

> Within the Revolution, everything; against the Revolution, nothing. Against the Revolution, nothing, because the Revolution has the right to exist, and no one shall oppose the right of the Revolution to exist. Inasmuch as the Revolution understands the interests of the people, inasmuch as the Revolution signifies the interests of the whole nation, no one can justly claim a right in opposition to the Revolution.
>
> (Castro 1962: 21)

Culture is a mass activity in Cuba and going to the public library is an everyday experience for many working-class Cubans, creating high levels of library membership, personal visits and circulation. According to *Cuba Cultural Statistics 1987* (Julia and Iglesias 1988: unpaginated), in 1987, Cuba had more than 4000 libraries, 328 of them public libraries, which was an increase from just 32 in 1964. The number of bookshops increased to 326 during the same period. Cuban public libraries had over 7 million titles, nearly 6 million of them books, which was an increase from 675,000 in 1964. This reflected an increase in the number of titles published in Cuba from 507 in 1959 to 2,315 in 1987, including 1961 books. A total of 41,934,000 copies of these titles, including 37,830,200 books, with an average of 18,114 copies per average edition, were produced in 1987. This amounted to 22.4 titles per 100,000 inhabitants and 4049 copies per 1000 inhabitants. Between 1980 and 1987, more than 800 titles were published in foreign languages, for a total of 28.2 million copies. In 1987, book sales totalled 10.6 million pesos, a 46 per cent increase over 1980. This was a remarkable achievement for a developing country that was subject to an economic blockade since 1962.

This level of book production was only made possible by committed state support. The Ministry of Culture has nine publishing houses: People and Education, Social Sciences, Scientific-Technical, Art and Literature, Cuban Letters, New People and Jose Marti (all of which belong to the Cuban Book Institute) and the Casa de las Americas publishing house. There are also other publishing houses such as the Communist Party's Political Publishing, the Union of Young Communists April Publishing and the Union of Writers and Artists publishing department. Taken together, they comprise a group of specialised entities whose production in 1987 accounted for 90 per cent of the titles published and 99 per cent of all books and booklets printed in Cuba.

Book production was impacted by the collapse of the Soviet Union when Cuba entered 'The Special Period in Times of Peace'. An estimated US$4 million in income from the capitalist world was lost during this period. In 1990, the total budget assigned to culture was 138.7 billion pesos, a reduction of 10.5 billion. This had a profound effect on cultural institutions, but no public libraries were closed, and not a single library worker lost their job. This is in stark contrast to the hundreds of public libraries that have been shuttered and the thousands of library workers who have been made redundant in the UK since the 2008 financial crisis.

How does the Vanguard library operate?

Having defined the Vanguard library under capitalism and socialism, we would now like to describe how this library operates in practice. The purpose of going into this level of detail is to provide a road map and blueprint for practitioners to construct their own Vanguard library. Some librarians do not know where to start this process; others believe that it is not possible unless the economic, social and political conditions are right. We make it clear in this chapter that a Vanguard library can be built in any place and at any time. The key components of this operation are strategy, structures, staffing and services and systems. Together, these form the base (forces and relations of production) of the Vanguard library, and this base shapes and determines the superstructure (ideology and organisational culture). In describing each of these core components, we illustrate them with real-life examples of currently existing Vanguard libraries operating in both capitalist and socialist societies.

Strategy

The strategy of the Vanguard library within a capitalist system is developed by taking a dialogical approach to engaging with the proletariat. The Vanguard library gathers community intelligence from the working class in order to understand their needs. The Vanguard library never assumes or second-guesses the needs of the proletariat and fully accepts that the working class is an expert in its own needs. As Mao pointed out,

> [o]ur cultural workers must serve the people with great enthusiasm and devotion, and they must link themselves with the masses, not divorce themselves from the masses. In order to do so, they must act in accordance with the needs and wishes of the masses. All work done for the masses must start from their needs and not from the desire of any individual, however well intentioned. It often happens that objectively the masses need a certain change, but subjectively they are not yet conscious of the need, not yet willing or determined to make the change. In such cases, we should wait patiently. We should not make the change until, through our work, most of the masses have become conscious of the need and are willing and determined to carry it out. Otherwise we shall isolate ourselves from the masses. There are two principles here: one is the actual needs of the masses rather than what we fancy they need, and the other is the wishes of the masses, who must make up their own minds instead of our making up their minds for them.
>
> (1991: 186–187)

A dialogical approach to strategy development was used by Thunder Bay Public Library (TBPL), Ontario, Canada to create a Strategic Plan for 2019–23. A series of community conversations (Harwood Institute 2016) were held across the city in 2018. These community conversations provided a safe space where working-class people could come together to talk about their aspirations, concerns and how they wanted their community to move forward. The typical community conversation had about 8 to 15 participants and lasted from between 90 minutes to 2 hours. A TBPL moderator guided the conversation using a discussion guide, which was developed by the Harwood Institute over a period of 25 years and tested and used in communities of all sizes and make-ups. These conversations were used as a means of gathering public knowledge, which is different to expert knowledge. Expert knowledge comes from expert or professional analysis. It often includes data, demographic and market studies, evidence-based decision-making and best practices. It is usually presented in expert or professional language. Public knowledge comes only from engaging in conversation with people in a community. Only the people within the community themselves can tell us their aspirations, concerns and how they see different facets of their community. It is usually in plain language that everyone can understand. This public knowledge helped TBPL ground the work of the library in the objective reality of the proletariat. This knowledge identified key issues of concern to people in language that people themselves use and it uncovered and generated a sense of common purpose for action in the community. This knowledge also helped set realistic goals for moving head and making change and made the work of TBPL more relevant and more impactful within the community.

These conversations were not about the library and what it does but about the lived experience and the material conditions of the working class. Questions such as 'What kind of a community do you want?' and 'What are the two or three most important issues or concerns when it comes to the community?' are useful in identifying the day-to-day challenges faced by working-class people. Questions such as 'What do you think is keeping us from making the progress we want?' and 'What are the kinds of things that could be done that would make a difference?' are useful in identifying what actions the proletariat thinks should be taken in response to these challenges. Questions such as 'If we came back together in six months or a year, what might you see that would be an indication that the things we talked about today were starting to happen?' are useful in helping the working class to identify success criteria which they can use to hold TBPL accountable for meeting community needs.

During these conversations, TBPL heard firsthand testimony from a wide range of working-class people about what it was like to live, work and study in Thunder Bay. These conversations were not filtered or censored in any way, and sometimes the views expressed were not shared by TBPL or other participants. The only requirement was that these views were expressed respectfully. TBPL hosted these conversations as platforms that enabled working-class people to say exactly what they thought and felt about a particular issue. There was no judgement by TBPL of these views because it was recognised that they reflected a lived reality. Thunder Bay is on the front line of the race war and the class struggle in Canada. It is a 'blue-collar' community with high levels of poverty and homelessness and has the highest per capita Indigenous population of any city in Canada. *Macleans* magazine has called out Thunder Bay as the 'race hate capital of Canada'. Given these realities, it is not surprising that racism, poverty and homelessness featured in every community conversation and became strategic objectives in the TBPL Strategic Plan for 2019–23:

- Challenge institutional and systemic racism by working with Indigenous peoples, visible minorities and white allies to pursue racial justice; decolonising the library service; developing policies, systems, collections and programs and recruiting a diverse staff who reflect the community we serve

- Mitigate the impact of homelessness and poverty by adopting a poverty, economic inequality and homelessness policy; providing free resources and removing barriers to access; and supporting people with mental health and addictions challenges

The Thunder Bay proletariat spoke out loud and clear about their needs, and TBPL listened, acknowledged and accepted their aspirations and concerns. Examples of how TBPL responded to these needs are given in the following sections on staffing structure, service structure, systems and culture.

The strategy of the Vanguard library within a socialist system is guided by the legacy of Marx, Engels and Lenin and considers the teachings of the October Revolution – which, under Lenin, changed the course of world history – decisive for its own strength and development. The Vanguard library combines two essential, fundamental, invaluable factors: the unity of the working class and a scientific doctrine and political-revolutionary philosophy: Marxism-Leninism. The main pillars of the Vanguard library in Cuba are working-class unity and Marxist-Leninism, the rule of merit, revolutionary virtues, modesty and close ties with the masses, from whom the library should never be separated, for these ties are what give the library its meaning, prestige, authority and strength.

In Cuba, the Vanguard library reflects the interests of the proletariat and meets their needs. Library workers do not use their professional status, education or qualifications to elevate or separate themselves from the working class. Library workers are fellow members of the proletariat and place themselves alongside or behind (in a supporting role) rather than ahead of the masses. They do not assume that they are experts in community needs because they accept that the working class are the experts in their own needs. The Vanguard library is never above the masses but always with the masses and in the hearts of the people. Authority does not come from being the Vanguard library; rather, the authority of the library always stems from the idea and the concept that the people have of the library.

Staffing structure

The staffing structure of the Vanguard library within a capitalist society is driven by the objectives within the strategic plan. At TBPL, this means recruiting a diverse staff who reflect the working-class population in the city. For example, before 2019, TBPL had no Indigenous staff, despite the fact that 15 per cent of the local community were Indigenous. In response to the 2019–2023 Strategic Plan objective to 'challenge institutional and systemic racism', TBPL created two new positions: Community Hub

Technician – Indigenous Relationships and Community Hub Librarian – Indigenous Relationships. As the job titles suggest, the main purpose of these positions was to build relationships between TBPL and the Indigenous community in Thunder Bay. For this to happen, it was critical that the people who held these positions had lived Indigenous experience.

The staffing structure of the Vanguard library within the socialist system is organic, and its internal life is developed on the basis of rigorous observation of rules that combine strict discipline with broad internal democracy, the exercise of collective leadership and individual responsibility and the practice of criticism and self-criticism of its own errors, all of which guarantee the purity and cohesion of its management and staff and the required unity of thought and action along with the greatest freedom of discussion and initiatives. In Cuba, this means that the Vanguard library operates according to the concepts of self-criticism and democratic centralism.

Self-criticism maintains that revolutionaries must always conduct rigorous self-evaluations in order to identify their errors and rectify them. Library workers must have the ability and power to be critical of not only themselves but also the vanguard and criticise those who are not prioritising and meeting the needs of the working class. If libraries are to provide the best service to the working class, they must undertake frequent self-criticisms. Democratic centralism, or 'freedom of discussion, unity of action', is the essence of democratic centralism. The Vanguard library must organise itself on this basis. Discussion and debate should be encouraged before a decision is reached, but after one has been made, everyone must follow the chosen line. There can be no localism. Everyone must carry out the directives as determined by the vanguard.

Service structure

The service structure of the Vanguard library within a capitalist society is driven by the objectives within the strategic plan. At TBPL, this means developing services, collections and programs that meet the needs of the working class. TBPL responded to the needs of the Indigenous community, as identified in the 2019–2023 Strategic Plan, by creating Indigenous Knowledge Centres (IKC) at all four libraries. Before these IKCs were developed, the library collections at TBPL did not reflect the history, culture or values of working-class Indigenous people. In designing the IKC's TBPL received guidance from the Indigenous Advisory Council (IAC), which was formed in response to another objective in the 2019–2023 Strategic Plan, to 'decolonize the library service'. The IAC gave working-class Indigenous people some agency over the decisions made by TBPL, which guaranteed that any suggestions or recommendations made by the IAC would be fully implemented. The IKCs were the first test of this commitment.

The IKCs are different from other collections at TBPL in that they are not arranged according to the Western linear worldview of knowledge which is reflected in the Dewey Decimal Classification (DDC) scheme. Within this scheme, every book is given a classification number from 000 to 999. For example, *The Pedagogy of the Oppressed* is classified at 370.115 (education – philosophy). The IKC collection, on the other hand, reflects the Indigenous worldview that knowledge is 'circular', and the books are categorised accordingly. For example, the books that are categorised as Aki (Land) in the IKC would be found at 346.711, 917.131 and 970.004 in the DDC scheme, and the books that are categorised as Kwe (Women) in the IKC would be found at 305.48, 323.119 and 977.004 in the DDC scheme. Here we can see that, whereas the DDC classification system tends to scatter books about the same subject throughout the library, the IKC categories are more holistic in that they gather together books about a particular issue. These different approaches reflect Western individualism (every book has its own place in the library) and Indigenous collectivism (every book is related to other books). The Indigenous worldview is similar to Marxism, which also considers that everything is interconnected.

The service structure of the Vanguard library in a socialist society channels its activities and guides its efforts throughout the process of building and developing socialism toward the construction of the technical-material base of communist society, the organisation and development of the economy and a constant increase in production and work productivity, so the material living conditions of the people are progressively improved. In Cuba, this means that the Vanguard library operates according to the concept of centralised planning. The Vanguard library – with input from workers and the community – sets targets for development and strives to achieve them via long-term plans. This may take the form of a Five-Year Plan, for example, which lays out in some detail what the Vanguard library plans to achieve in the coming five-year period. This plan also identifies the resources required to achieve the planned outcomes. The Vanguard library is required to report its progress against targets set in the plan, and these can be used by the working class to hold the library accountable for its performance.

Systems

The systems of the Vanguard library within a capitalist society are driven by the objectives within the strategic plan. At TBPL, this means providing free resources and removing barriers to access. For example, up until 2019, TBPL imposed a financial penalty on people who did not return their books on time, even though research indicated that library fines were a major economic barrier for working-class people who are on low or no incomes. Given that mitigating poverty and homelessness is a strategic objective of the 2019–2023 Strategic Plan, TBPL responded by eliminating fines in early 2020. This is a good example of TBPL using the evidence provided by lived experience and material conditions to change its systems. Another example is related to the behaviour policy at TBPL. At one time, this was worded in such a way that any patron who the staff suspected of being intoxicated (by alcohol or drugs) was automatically excluded from the library. This had a disproportionate impact on the Indigenous community who, because of the damage done to them by generations of settler-colonial policies and practices, experience high levels of alcoholism and addictions. For many Indigenous people, this is how they cope with living in a capitalist society that has stolen their land and attempted to destroy their culture. Recognising this lived reality, TBPL amended its behaviour policy in 2020 to enable patrons who are intoxicated to use the library as long as their behaviour is not a problem for staff or other patrons.

The systems of the Vanguard library within a socialist society provide leadership that unites, organises, guides and orients the working class and social organisations in their activities to bring to fruition their main programmatic aim; the building of a communist society, freed forever of all kinds of exploitation, in which men are equals, friends and comrades. In Cuba, this means that the Vanguard library operates according to the concept of emancipation. In Marxism, emancipation is at the opposite pole of alienation. If alienation is the separation of the human from their humanity, then emancipation is their realisation of this humanity. It is the full realisation of human needs. The Vanguard library can aid emancipation by tailoring its services to meet the needs of the working class and other exploited strata. In doing so, the Vanguard library assists in the process of developing the 'new socialist man' (Guevara 1965).

Ideology and organisational culture

The organisational culture of the Vanguard library within a capitalist society reflects Marx's hierarchy of needs, which was later endorsed by Maslow (1943). In doing so, it pays particular attention to basic needs and those who have the greatest needs. In capitalist societies, public libraries are often used the most by people who need them the least and used the least by people who need them the most (Muddiman et al. 1999). The ideology of the Vanguard library aims to reverse this paradigm by ensuring that the people who need libraries the most (proletariat) use them the most and the people who need them the least (bourgeoisie) use them the least. Given that having somewhere to live is a basic need and homelessness is a priority within the Strategic Plan for 2019–2023, TBPL took a number of actions in response to this need. For example, TBPL formed partnerships with a range of health and welfare services to provide street nurses, HIV testing and social workers in the library. This means that homeless people can now access mental and physical health care at the point of need and be connected with housing and other agencies that can assist in meeting their basic needs. In addition, given that many government and support services are now only available online, TBPL provided technology for loan to homeless people to help bridge the digital divide.

Technology has a role to play in the Vanguard library. However, Marxists regard technology as a means to an end rather than just an end in itself. Library technology is sometimes pointed to as evidence that public libraries have evolved and changed and kept up with the times. We agree that technology is a means of *modernising* the public library, but this is not necessarily the same thing as *changing* or *transforming* the library. In other words, a Traditional library may deploy lots of shiny new technology while remaining fundamentally unchanged in terms of its purpose and whose interest it serves. This points to one of the capitalist interpretations of the public library which focuses only on *what* the library does and *how* it does it (Feather 2013; Webster 2014). Technology is used by the Vanguard library to meet the needs of the working class. The Bridging the Digital Divide project at TBPL is a good example of this. The role of technology in promoting social justice has become evident and amplified in the COVID 19–era digitised world.

While TBPL is focused on the basic needs of the working-class community, it also addresses some of their higher-level needs as well. In this regard, TBPL formed a partnership with Anishnabek Employment and Training Services (AETS) to meet the employment and training needs of the working-class Indigenous community. AETS is co-located in one of TBPL's main downtown libraries, which means that its Indigenous clients also have access to all the free resources that TBPL provides. In return, TBPL has seen an increase in the number of Indigenous people who visit the library, take out a membership card, use services and borrow materials.

The organisational culture of the Vanguard library in Cuba reflects the ideology of the socialist state, which means that the library is the organised vanguard of the working class, that on the basis of a free and voluntary association, brings together the best of the people, chosen from among the most outstanding workers, who, guided by Marxism-Leninism, are actively trying to build socialism and achieve the objectives of communism. At the same time, the Vanguard library emphasises consciousness-raising and ideological preparation of the masses so they are educated in the values of communist morality; it helps create the new man – who, stripped of bourgeois and petit-bourgeois morality and ideology (based on individualism and egotism), governs his conduct by the noblest principles of collectivism, self-sacrifice, love of work, hatred of parasitism and the fraternal spirit of cooperation and solidarity among all the members of society and among the socialist countries and workers and peoples throughout the world.

Socialism 'should be seen as an emancipatory process, as a change and reconstruction of economic, political, social, and cultural relations with the intention of eliminating alienation by means of social inclusion and decentralization of power' (Prieto 2010: 96–97). Culture plays a role in satisfying some of humankind's basic needs and creating values that distinguish worker from consumer, citizen from client, real person from instrumental one. In summary, the Vanguard library in Cuba develops all its activities based on the following fundamental principles:

1 Absolute fidelity to the interests of the working class
2 Firmness in the all-out struggle against the capitalist regime and all forms of exploitation of man
3 Fidelity to Marxism-Leninism as its vanguard theory and guide for action, which it strives to apply creatively in the concrete conditions of the working class and develop on the basis of their own experiences, defending this theory against all rightist and leftist deviations and against the attacks and deformations of the bourgeois theorists, revisionist and pseudo-Marxist dogmatists
4 Fidelity to proletarian internationalism, combined with the highest spirit of socialist patriotism and the struggle against all manifestations of chauvinism and petty nationalism
5 Close ties with the masses whom it guides and directs while learning from them, starting with the principle that the masses constitute an inexhaustible source of experience, values and strength

The fifth principle reflects Paulo Freire's dialogical approach in which the teacher (Vanguard library) educates the students (proletariat) and, in turn, learns from them. Instead of simply 'banking' the experience, values and strength of the Vanguard library into the 'empty heads' of the working class, the Vanguard library relates the experience, values and strength of the proletariat to Marxism in order to raise their level of class consciousness. In Cuba, participation in artistic production has been actively encouraged in a bid to develop individual and social consciousness. This required a complete overhaul of the education system, the construction of new schools and public libraries and the training of tens of thousands of art teachers and library workers, representing a political and economic commitment that remains unsurpassed in any other part of the world.

Conclusion

The Vanguard library exists to advance the cause of the working class. Its twin pillars are proletarian unity and Marxist-Leninist philosophy. The road map and blueprint which we propose in this chapter are, like the recommendations in the *Communist Manifesto* (Marx and Engels 1971), a call to action. They call on librarians everywhere to improve their services for the working class, and they indicate how this can be done. These measures include, but are not limited to, the following:

- Developing strategies and policies, staffing, services, systems and culture that meet the needs of the working class
- Strategies: a redesign of the library from the ground up that provides a hospitable environment for the working class
- Policies: giving the working class a leading role in shaping the library services, from selecting the staff and choosing the books to the opening hours and rules
- Staffing: giving preference to working-class people with lived experience of class oppression when hiring staff
- Services: providing programmes, services and collections which reflect working-class history and culture
- Culture: ensuring that the organisational culture ('the way we do things around here') is driven by working-class values and consciousness

The Vanguard library can exist under capitalism and socialism. Its leadership role can contribute towards building a fairer, more equal society and developing working-class consciousness in preparation for socialism and the 'new man'. As such, the Vanguard library answers Marx's clarion call that we should not only seek to understand the world but also change it for the emancipation of all.

References

Benedetti, M. (1968) 'On the Relations between the Man of Action and the Intellectual', *Revolucion y Cultura*/4, 15 February.
Bevan, A. (1952) *In Place of Fear*. London: Simon and Schuster.
Castro, F. (1962) *Words to the Intellectuals*. Havana: Ministry of Foreign Relations.

―――― (1994) *Che: A Memoir by Fidel Castro*. Melbourne: Ocean Press.
Craven, D. (2006) *Art and Revolution in Latin America 1910–1990*. New Haven, CT and London: Yale University Press.
Cuban Book Institute (1968) *Cultural Congress of Havana: Meeting of Intellectuals from All the World on Problems of Asia, Africa and Latin America*. Havana: Cuban Book Institute.
―――― (1971) *First Congress on Education and Culture*. Havana: Cuban Book Institute.
Dalton, R. et al. (1969) 'Ten Years of Revolution: The Intellectual and Society', *Casa de Las Americas*, 10/56, October.
Dobler, F. (1983) 'The Modern Library System', in V. I. Lenin (ed.) *Lenin and Library Organisation*, pp. 62–65. Moscow: Progress Publishers.
Feather, J. (2013) *The Information Society: A Study of Continuity and Change*. London: Facet Publishing.
Freire, P. (1979) *Pedagogy of the Oppressed*. New York: Continuum.
Gordon-Nesbitt, R. (2015) *To Defend the Revolution Is to Defend Culture: The Cultural Policy of the Cuban Revolution*. Oakland: PM Press.
Guevara, E. (1965) 'Socialism and Man in Cuba', *Marcha*, 12 March.
Harwood Institute (2016) *Public Innovators Lab Guide*. Harwood: The Institute for Public Innovation.
Julia, M. and Iglesias, T. (1988) *Cuba Cultural Statistics 1987*. Havana: Editorial de Ciencias Sociales.
Lenin, V. (1960) *On Socialist Culture and Ideology*. Moscow: Foreign Languages Publishing House.
Mao-Tse-Tung (1991) *Selected Works of Mao-Tse-Tung*, Vol. 3. Beijing: People's Publishing House.
Marx, K. and Engels, F. (1971) *Communist Manifesto*. Moscow: Progress Publishers.
Maslow, A. (1943) 'A Theory of Human Motivation', *Psychological Review*, 50/4: 370–396.
Morton, H. V. (1932) *In Search of Wales*. London: Methuen.
Muddiman, D. et al. (1999) *Open to All? The Public Library and Social Exclusion*. London: Resource.
National Council of Culture (1963) *Draft of the 1963 Cultural Plan*. Havana: National Council of Culture.
Pateman, J. and Pateman, J. (2019) *Managing Cultural Change in Public Libraries*. London: Routledge.
Prieto, M. (2010) 'Looking at Cuba Today: Four Assumptions and Six Intertwined Problems', *Socialism and Democracy*, 24/1.
Provincial Council of Culture (1961) *Culture for the People*. Havana: Provincial Council of Culture.
Retamar, R. (1966) 'Towards a Revolutionary Intelligentsia in Cuba', in *Cuba Defendida*. Havana: Casa De Las Americas.
Rose, J. (2002) *The Intellectual Life of the British Working Classes*. New Haven: Yale University Press.

Sanchez Vasquez, A. (1973) *Art and Society: Essays in Marxist Aesthetics*. London: Merlin Press.

Sarusky, J. and Mosquera, G. (1979) *The Cultural Policy of Cuba*. Paris: UNESCO.

Sochor, Z. (1988) *Revolution and Culture: The Bogdanov-Lenin Controversy*. Ithaca, NY and London: Cornell University Press.

Webster, F. (2014) *Theories of the Information Society*. London: Routledge.

Wesker, A. (1969) 'Aie Cuba! Aie Cuba!', *Envoy*, November.

6 Conclusion

This book has brought together the history, theory and practice of Marxism and public libraries. In the spirit of Marxism, it did so not with the aim of merely understanding public libraries but with the aim of changing them. This book utilised Marxism as a guide to create the blueprint for a library that truly serves the public, which, in its most genuine sense, means the working class. Having done that, it is now useful to summarise the main points.

The first chapter defined *Marxism* and *public library*. Whilst acknowledging that both concepts are complex and contested, it identified essential principles for each. Marxism is a scientific theory for critically examining society and its historical laws of development. It is also a revolutionary doctrine of the fighting working class. Marxism maintains that the class struggle culminates in the dictatorship of the proletariat, a system of working-class rule that is a prelude to the full construction of socialism and communism. The essential analytical tool of Marxism is *class*. Contrary to the views of its critics, however, Marxism does not ignore the importance of "identities" such as race and gender. It does not ignore the intersectional character of various forms of oppression. It does not ignore the role of culture and ideology in capitalism. It does, however, highlight the central importance of class in understanding and dealing with these issues.

The public library, in its most basic meaning, is a library that serves everyone in society. There have been three interpretations of this ambiguous concept. The original one considers it to be a cultural expression of class power. As a power institution, it serves the cultural development of a definite class whilst suppressing the culture of another class. A second, more widespread interpretation considers the public library merely as an *information provider*. It ignores the question of *whose* rule is embodied in the institution, and it concentrates primarily on *the way the service is delivered*. The third interpretation disregards broadening the public library into a concept that is completely general, comprehensive and positive. It associates the public library with the promotion of desirable ideals like 'democracy', 'freedom' and 'inclusion'. The second and third interpretations obscure the class content of the public library, and that is why they are promoted by the ideologists of capitalism. These people want to hide the fact that modern public libraries exclude the working masses.

Chapter 2 established the Marxist interpretation of the public library. It argued, in broad agreement with the original interpretation, that the concept has a class character. It is a cultural manifestation of the power of a definite class. The public library serves the ruling class whilst suppressing the subjugated classes. Throughout history, there are ancient, feudal, capitalist, socialist and communist public libraries.

As a cultural category, situated within the superstructure of society, the public library is shaped and determined by the economic base. It is also relatively autonomous. It is able, particularly when the economic system is unstable – to operate independently and even against the prevailing economic and class relations. The Community-Led and Needs-Based public libraries are concrete examples of this.

The view, spread by bourgeois theorists, that public libraries support and embody democracy, freedom and equality is groundless. Depending on the class character of the public library in question, they may either support or oppose these ideals for particular classes.

The public librarian is a historical category. Trained library professionals emerged as a necessity under capitalism, and they remain necessary under socialism. But as technological advancements simplify the key library functions, these professionals will gradually become superfluous, and the popular masses will themselves manage the libraries under communism.

Chapter 3 examined V. I. Lenin's work in establishing the theoretical foundations of the Marxist-Leninist socialist public library service. Lenin argued that public libraries are a leading force in developing the cultural, educational, technical and scientific levels of the working masses under socialism. He oversaw the creation of an integrated, centralised, state-controlled library service in the world's first socialist state. This model has served as a basic template for all socialist countries. Most crucially, Lenin established the principles of fidelity to the working class and Marxism-Leninism as the founding tenets of Marxist librarianship.

Chapter 4 focused on North Korea's socialist public library system. Kim Il-Sung played a leading role in developing this service. The Marxist-Leninist and North Korean public libraries are similar in that they both serve the construction of socialism and communism. Based as it was upon the Marxist-inspired *Juche* idea, however, the DPRK system differs from the Marxist-Leninist model in several respects. The country's public libraries are (1) more focused on ideology, (2) they seek to establish a monolithic

Conclusion   119

ideological system of total unity, (3) they are more isolated from foreign libraries, (4) they are more uniform in design and organisation and (5) they focus more on idolising the Great Leader over the party. The key discovery of Juche is that a workers' library can be built under any circumstances, regardless of the objective conditions, so long as the library service is armed with the revolutionary outlook and leadership of the working class.

Chapter 5 considered the role of the Vanguard library in capitalist and socialist societies. That the Vanguard library is possible under capitalism was proved by the miners' libraries that emerged on the South Wales coalfields in the early twentieth century. These libraries were paid for and operated by the miners themselves and met the educational and cultural needs of the industrial working class. The Vanguard library under socialism played a critical role after the triumph of the revolution in Cuba in 1959. The successful campaign to eradicate illiteracy in just one year created an insatiable demand for books and a network of libraries was developed throughout the island, closing the divide between rural and urban areas and peoples. In whatever context, the leadership role of the Vanguard library is to raise working-class consciousness by educating workers (and thereby boost economic production) and by creating a 'new man' imbued with socialist ideology. The twin pillars of the Vanguard library are the unity of the proletariat and Marxism-Leninism. These are reflected in the strategy, structures, systems and organisational culture of the Vanguard library.

Marxism has proved itself as an effective theory for understanding and perfecting public libraries. Like any science, however, Marxism cannot stand still. It requires constant development in light of new discoveries and environmental changes. This means that it would be a violation of Marxism to rest content with the theories and frameworks outline here. It would be a violation of Marxism to become a dogmatist and cling to the letter over the reality. Scientific progress demands that one must always observe the actual concrete reality and adjust the theory in order to make sense of this reality. That is what being a Marxist means. That is why librarians should carry forward this book's findings, develop them, enrich them and struggle to build a truly revolutionary vanguard public library service, one that is worthy of the fighting working class.

Index

American-Swiss library system 51–53
ancient public libraries 6, 21–29, 35–39

Castro, Fidel 93, 101, 104
censorship 3, 14, 45
class consciousness 32, 48–49, 95–102, 113–114
class power 6–7, 22, 60, 117
class struggle 10–14, 21, 95–97, 117
Communist Party of the Soviet Union 44
community-led library 25–27, 30–31, 35–38, 95
critical theory 9–14
Cuban libraries 68, 71, 86–88, 92–96, 100–105, 108–113
cultural revolution 48–49, 96

dialectical materialism 4–5, 13–14, 27
dictatorship of the proletariat 5, 14, 29, 35, 103

Engels, Frederick 23–30, 39–48, 58–67, 71–74, 98–100, 108–114

Freire, Paulo 94–95

Grand People's Study House 72–73, 81–85
Guevara, Che 96, 102, 111

historical materialism 5, 29

intersectionality 9–14

Juche idea 17, 71–78, 80–88, 90

Kim Il-Sung 17, 73–81, 83–91

Lenin, Vladimir 44–52, 53–61, 62–70
Lenin State Library 67

Mao-Tse-Tung 1, 94, 106
Marx, Karl 13–17, 48, 58, 62–70, 97–98, 100
Marxism-Leninism 4–6, 12–17, 62–63, 68–76, 85–86, 112–113
miners' libraries 97–99

needs-based library 26–27, 30–31, 35–38, 95
neo-liberalism 10, 35, 95

October Socialist Revolution 47–50

Socialist public library 45–47, 53–60, 65–69, 71–79, 82–91
Stalin, Joseph 1, 58, 74

traditional library 25–29, 35, 94–95, 112

Vanguardism 5, 50, 92

workers' libraries 2, 39, 53
Workers' Party of Korea 72